CHALLENGING
MULTIRACIAL
IDENTITY

CHALLENGING MULTIRACIAL IDENTITY

Rainier Spencer

LYNNE
RIENNER
PUBLISHERS

BOULDER
LONDON

Published in the United States of America in 2006 by
Lynne Rienner Publishers, Inc.
1800 30th Street, Boulder, Colorado 80301
www.rienner.com

and in the United Kingdom by
Lynne Rienner Publishers, Inc.
3 Henrietta Street, Covent Garden, London WC2E 8LU

Library of Congress Cataloging-in-Publication Data
Spencer, Rainier.
    Challenging multiracial identity / Rainier Spencer.
        p. cm.
    Includes bibliographical references and index.
    ISBN-13: 978-1-58826-424-4 (hardcover : alk. paper)
    ISBN-10: 1-58826-424-6 (hardcover : alk. paper)
    1. Racially mixed people—Race identity. 2. Racially mixed people—Race identity—United
States. 3. Race—Social aspects. 4. Race—Social aspects—United States. I. Title.
HT1523.S59 2006
305.8—dc22

                                                                        2006011919

British Cataloguing in Publication Data
A Cataloguing in Publication record for this book
is available from the British Library.

Printed and bound in the United States of America

⊗   The paper used in this publication meets the requirements
     of the American National Standard for Permanence of
     Paper for Printed Library Materials Z39.48-1992.

5   4   3   2   1

To Jackie

Contents

Acknowledgments

When I consider those who have contributed to the publication of *Challenging Multiracial Identity,* there are at least two divisions I make. The first group includes those who have been responsible in some way or other for my being able to work on the project at all. The second group includes those whose specific assistance somewhere along the line from concept to publication I want to mention.

First and foremost, I expressly include Him whose grace and peace sustain me through all the peaks and valleys of life.

In terms of the first group, I would like to acknowledge the following persons: my wife, Jackie, who deserves far more than I could ever give her; Patricia Penn Hilden, to whom I will be indebted my entire professional life; and Maile, Paula, and Tiara Suehiro, for true friendship.

As for the second group, I would like to thank Lynne Rienner Publishers, and especially Lynne herself for the confidence and patience she has so graciously shown me in this endeavor. Other staff members of Lynne Rienner Publishers I want to thank specifically are Lisa Tulchin, Karen Schneider, and Lesli Athanasoulis. I would also like to acknowledge a former staff member of Lynne Rienner Publishers, Bridget Julian, who in several ways stands at the point of this book's very conception. Lynne Rienner Publishers also engaged a number of talented individuals whose contributions have enhanced this project. These individuals include the peer reviewers, whose comments and helpful criticism I appreciate. I am also especially grateful to Kerry Ann Rockquemore, who truly challenged me to extend myself in finalizing the manuscript. And, this book benefited enormously from the outstanding copyediting talents of Jason Cook.

Finally, I thank all those whose work in this field of study, whether pioneering or contemporary, has contributed in some way or other to the publication of this book.

—*Rainier Spencer*

CHALLENGING MULTIRACIAL IDENTITY

Introduction:
Expecting Excellence in the Field of
Multiracial Identity Studies

They believe popular folktales and follow the crowd as their teachers,
ignoring the adage that the many are bad, the good are few.
—Heraclitus (fragment)[1]

It is not nearly as difficult today as it was ten or fifteen years ago to find scholarly books and journal articles on the subject of multiracial identity.[2] As someone who truly lamented the dearth of such resources when I was a graduate student writing my dissertation, it is with deep humility and a warm gladness that I make note of the fact that my own published work now serves as the kind of resource for students and scholars today that was not so readily available to me at the time. Today there are considerably more resources, more single-authored books, more anthologies, and more journal articles than in those early days, not so very long ago, when the field was only beginning to come into existence. Having noted this positive development, however, it is necessary as well to take stock of this maturing academic field of study and to assess it with an objective eye. The time has come to take an honest look at where multiracial identity studies is and where it is going, a no-holds-barred examination of the field. It is no exaggeration to state that nothing less than the scholarly integrity of multiracial identity studies is potentially at stake in such an exercise; and I hope that the endeavor will ultimately be a collective one, with this book providing but one of several needed correctives.

While there may be a number of equally plausible ways to organize the field of multiracial identity studies, I am choosing here to make a basic, first-order division based on acceptance or nonacceptance of the idea of multiracial identity as constituting a real, useful, and logically

persuasive means of assigning human beings to racial (including multiracial) groups. Such a division results generally in a branch that advocates multiracial identity on the one hand, and a branch that refutes the
notions of race and multirace on the other. The former group tends to
operate from the assumption, necessitated by its fundamental position
(whether admitted openly or not), that biological race exists as a physical reality, while the latter tends to engage in what I term a metatheoretical approach to analysis, an approach that seeks to problematize biological race and its various reifications but that is sometimes faulted as
being unsympathetic to people's emotional and psychological needs.[3] I
have myself been criticized on this last point. This branch studies race
as a false consciousness that has given rise to the additional fallacy of
multiracial identity, and strives to examine and understand the expression of that identity in historical as well as contemporary contexts, while
the former group assumes that multirace (and, by extension, race) is a
biological reality, and urges federal recognition of multiracial identity.
In a very close analogy, the situation is akin to that of an academic field
of flat-Earth theory in which one side conducts metatheoretical analyses
of people's fallacious beliefs in a flat Earth and the implications thereof,
while the other side argues that Earth is indeed flat.

There has been since the early 1990s what might be termed a
"movement" of sorts, focused on the ultimate goal of adding a multiracial category to the official US racial designations authorized by the
Office of Management and Budget (OMB).[4] The increase in multiracial-
related scholarly publishing that I made reference to earlier may be
traced to this same beginning point. Thus, one might refer usefully to an
ongoing debate between "promovement" actors on one side and "anti-
movement" actors on the other. Of course, there are other terms one
might employ, and indeed I will make reference to different terminolo-
gies and characterizations throughout this book, but the basic division
will generally always be the same—those arguing for acceptance of
multiracial identity on one side, and those, in the context of racial skep-
ticism, arguing against such recognition on the other.

The debate has not always been between dueling groups of scholars,
however. In the early to middle 1990s the state of affairs tended in large
measure to find nonscholar activists who favored multiracial identity
(with a few scholars among their ranks) engaged in debate with scholars
who opposed them. These debates often took place in newspapers, in
popular magazines such as *Ebony, Emerge, Newsweek,* and *Time,* and in
more obscure, multiracial-oriented magazines such as *Interrace* and
New People. But with the flowering of scholarly publishing that has

taken place recently and that promises to continue, promovement scholars are largely displacing the activists from the debate scene.[5] And this is certainly a good thing, since the nonscholar activists were usually, if not always, simply not prepared intellectually to engage in the kind of rigorous and extensive logical dialectic necessary to address adequately questions such as this book will take up, for instance. Rather, simple raw emotion tended to rule the day in their case. Thus, pro–multiracial identity activists such as Susan Graham and Carlos Fernández have been supplanted by pro–multiracial identity scholars such as G. Reginald Daniel and Kathleen Korgen. One of the questions this book shall consider is whether the addition of scholars to the voices of those favoring recognition of multiracial identity has led to a significant improvement in the intellectual merit of the arguments raised in support of that particular position. My thesis is that as of yet it has not, and I shall be arguing this point throughout the book.

In carrying out this goal I shall not mince my words, as I am attempting sincerely to address what I consider serious deficiencies that serve to reduce the consistency and scholarly weight of multiracial identity studies as a whole. Several points I shall make, particularly regarding activist white mothers and white female academics writing in support of multiracial identity, might be received as shocking by some. The importance of making those points far outweighs the tact factor in my view, however. My basic position is that the most significant problem in regard to multiracial identity studies is the consistently inadequate performance of academics who write from the advocacy position.

I open therefore with the quite matter-of-fact observation that scholarly writing on the multiracial identity advocacy side tends to be inconsistent and error-filled. As someone who has, I hope, contributed to the field in a small but positive way, I lament what I consider to be the far too numerous cases of scholarly carelessness and outright sloppiness in the work of those writing in support of multiracial identity. In addition, several aspects of the promovement position—the influence of activist white mothers, and claims of first-generation multiracial identity, for instance—whether purposely or not, are supportive of a move toward a revised racial paradigm in the United States, a paradigm whose disturbing implications I shall address in Chapter 4.

This book represents an attempt to outline the parameters of the problem and to issue a challenge to academics sympathetic to the promovement stance—a challenge to publish work that passes minimal scholarly muster in order that a true dialectical debate can occur within this field of study between opposing philosophical positions, each possessing appropriate intellectual rigor and merit. As we shall see, such is demonstrably not the case in the current moment. I acknowledge that this is a strong criticism, but I see no reason to avoid calling into question that which should be questioned. Our unwillingness to point out poor-quality scholarship on multiracial identity when we encounter it is what has led to the present situation, in which people feel free to enter the subdiscipline and publish work that would be laughed out of most other fields of study.

While critiquing the inadequacies of arguments for multiracial identity in general, I shall focus on arguments for US black/white multiracial identity in particular. Because of their history over the past nearly four hundred years, Afro-Americans are one of the most (if not *the* most) genetically mixed populations in the United States. If multiracial identity were in fact to refer to something real, Afro-Americans—essentially all of them—would be multiracial. However, since advocates of multiracial identity expressly reject the inclusion of the general Afro-American population within the ranks of those qualifying for the exclusionary status of multiracial identity, the Afro-American case presents an excellent opportunity to assess the intellectual validity of the multiracial position. I want to acknowledge, therefore—up front and unequivocally—that this book is a completely unapologetic polemic against the notion of US black/white multiracial identity, particularly what is known as first-generation identity, and against published work to date that supports it.

Since its emergence in the early 1990s, the multiracial identity movement has been essentially motivated, propelled, and dominated by emotion. This emotion was provided initially by white mothers (primarily of black/white children), but has now been appropriated by the academics, who have displaced the activists from the debate scene. This is not to say that academics writing in support of multiracial identity today sound no different than the nonscholar activists they have since replaced. Indeed, newer scholarly trappings have given the old, emotional arguments of those activists a different flavor, but the intellectual merit and the conclusions of the new arguments remain the same as those of the old. As we shall see, one need not delve far beneath the surface of proidentity scholarship—in many cases, delving below the surface is not necessary at all—to detect a clear, emotionalistic bias that delegitimizes what ought to be solid research.

What is apparent is that on the whole, academics who write in support of multiracial identity are caught up in the very same emotionalism that enthralled the activists, an emotionalism that serves to cloud academic judgment and to lend uncorrected bias to scholarly work. As a result, that work has too often taken on the form of a crusade for multiracial identity, especially black/white multiracial identity, and especially for children. There is a double concern with work that takes this kind of turn. On the one hand, as I have indicated, its overly emotional character leads to bias that its adherents fail apparently to see; and on the other hand it tends to infantilize the population supposedly being *helped.*

Jill Olumide takes appropriate aim at the crusader character of such work when she observes that "claims to act on behalf of, or in the interests of, a whole socially identified group of people (black people; women; the oppressed; the poor; the 'natives') are redolent of imperialistic declarations of intent. . . . There is a kind of chauvinism which prevents the defined from exercising autonomy."[6] Similarly, discussing multiracial advocacy organizations, Laurie Mengel is concerned that "while some of the work done by White monoracials has given some mixed race people the tools and vocabularies from which to work and explore a collective voice, these organizations all characterize multiracial individuals as voiceless, disempowered, unformed persons—children—who need the authority of a White monoracial adult to speak for them."[7] When one adds the seemingly authoritative writings of proidentity academics to Mengel's point concerning the nonscholar activists who populate these organizations, the infantilization is broadened that much more. Of significant interest as well is the fact that it is monoracial white adults who are producing much of this academic writing.

In undertaking this assessment of proidentity scholarship, I have made a concerted effort to consider newer scholarly publications, as the first wave of material coming out of the early to middle 1990s has been fairly well reviewed and analyzed already. Therefore the reader will not find references to the major anthologies of that earlier period: the two edited by Maria Root and the one edited by Naomi Zack.[8] In that sense, this book itself serves as an illustration of the fact that multiracial identity studies has moved past its embryonic stage, past the Root and Zack anthologies, past the OMB's 1997 decision on revising federal racial categorization. One of this book's unique contributions, therefore, is its focused examination of where proidentity academic research is now heading.

Toward this end I have endeavored to review proidentity work published since the end of the 1990s. Where I do include older work, that work was published in more obscure venues (such as law, for instance) and was not part of the general debate in the United States during the time it was published. Moreover, I am focusing in particular on single-authored books, as such projects should be more comprehensive, should be more thorough, and should represent the best the field has to offer. While scholarly journals and anthologies often contain cutting-edge work, it seems to me that single-authored books offer (or should, at least) more in-depth analysis on the given subject, as well as a continuous and unified thread of thought from beginning to end. Additionally, because scholarly books are often easier to obtain and far more widely read than journal articles, by both academics and nonacademics alike, there is a power they thereby possess that is unmatched by the latter venue, even where the research itself might be superior.

In the chapters that follow, we will find ourselves returning often to four single-authored books—three interview studies by self-identified white women and one theoretical work by a self-identified multiracial male—that are in my view the top recent works produced by academics writing in support of multiracial identity. In addition, these four books are themselves centered either fully or in large measure on black/white multiracial identity, which is my interest as well. They provide excellent examples of what the proidentity perspective has to say today, and of how well the perspective is supported by valid evidence, solid research, and compelling argumentation. In addition to these four texts, I shall examine other recent work by proidentity writers in the form of books, anthology chapters, and journal articles.

In Chapter 1, I evaluate three recent, book-length interview studies that concern themselves either wholly or very substantially with black/white multiracial identity. The fact that as many as three such texts were published between 1999 and 2001 is, quite frankly, phenomenal, and I consider it essential to undertake a comparison of them. All three of these texts take the position, which will prove relevant to discussions in Chapters 3 and 4, that the younger generation of Americans of mixed ancestry has made an ideological shift toward explicit multiracial identity.

In undertaking this evaluation, I look at how the authors of these three studies compiled their interview subjects, how representative those subjects are of multiracials (in particular of black/white multiracials) in the United States, and whether the generalizations made to the broader populations of US multiracials are justified. Surprisingly, or perhaps unsurprisingly, these studies are very similar in a number of key respects that relate directly to my earlier comments regarding emotionalism and the bias it generates. In Chapter 1 we shall become familiar with these three authors, who will remain prominent throughout the remaining chapters as well.

From there we move to an appraisal of how two important fields of inquiry—psychology and sociology—tend to engage the issue of multiracial identity advocacy. Chapter 2 exposes the ways in which practitioners of psychology and sociology especially—in regard to multiracial identity specifically—engage in various kinds of evasive academic gymnastics to conceal not only the fact that they believe in biological race, but also the fact that biological race is absolutely central to their scholarly work. Beyond this, I investigate what I characterize as the neo- or reversed-pathology trope of multiracial identity, in which proidentity academics assert that black/white persons must receive specific psychological intervention so as to ensure the development of a healthy multiracial identity. Another aspect of this trope is an odd culture of victimization in which these academics insist that black/white children have a catalog of congenital special needs that must be addressed.

In Chapter 3, I examine the status of the 1967 Supreme Court decision *Loving v. Commonwealth of Virginia,* which struck down state laws against interracial marriage. I argue that this decision constitutes one of the central myths of the multiracial identity movement, and that it has not been shown to have had any of the direct and paradigm-altering effects that are attributed to it so routinely. In concert with the *Loving* legend, I also question the notion of a biracial baby boom as having taken place because of *Loving.* These positions in particular involve the restating by proidentity scholars, in newer academic garb, of older activist arguments. Chapter 3 also tackles an issue that has for too long been kept on the fringes of the multiracial identity debate—the place of white mothers in indoctrinating their black/white children to a multiracial identity, and whether that manner of indoctrination is any different than the indoctrination of black/white children to a black identity. This latter issue will be relevant to the discussion of the practical effects of a new multiracial identity in the successive chapter.

The proidentity school's emerging theoretical model is the notion of first-generation black/white multiracial identity, which is the subject of Chapter 4. This model involves deciding selectively which Afro-Americans are multiracial and which Afro-Americans are seemingly not; as such, the model works to erase the rich heterogeneity of the Afro-American past. Several key topics from the previous chapters come together in Chapter 4, as I consider the first-generation argument from both theoretical and practical perspectives. In this chapter I endeavor to demonstrate that the first-generation argument on the one hand is insupportable logically, and on the other represents a threat to install an altered American racial paradigm in which Afro-Americans would be even more isolated and powerless than under the current paradigm.

Chapter 5 serves as a brief postscript and summarizes the themes addressed in the book, suggesting that there is much work to do in order to bridge the current gap that exists within multiracial identity studies between metatheoretical academics on the one hand and proidentity academics on the other. It sketches the road forward, and suggests that proidentity academics should eschew the emotion-laden and misplaced arguments of the nonscholar activists, and instead focus on producing the kind of top-quality academic work that will benefit us all, regardless of which side of the field we inhabit. In that sense, the title of this book, *Challenging Multiracial Identity,* may be read two ways: as a general challenge to the concept of multiracial identity, and as a specific challenge to proidentity academics to do what is required in order to join metatheorists as higher-level, objective observers and analysts of the multiracial identity phenomenon, instead of continuing to merely be part of the object of study itself.

Notes

1. Philip Wheelwright, ed., *The Presocratics* (New York: Macmillan, 1985), 76.

2. Race terms in this book are always a reference to people's misguided belief in biological race and the US racial paradigm. Given that my topic concerns the notion of racially mixed people in the United States, my use of such terms is necessary as I endeavor to engage the debate using the linguistic tools currently at our disposal. Race terms in this text, therefore, should always be read as if preceded by the words "so-called." The only alternatives would have been to utilize far too many italicizations or to deploy cumbersome phraseology such as "persons who are perceived as, or who consider themselves to be, black" (or "white," "black/white," "multiracial," etc.), either of which would have been unacceptably distracting from the text itself.

3. Rainier Spencer, "Assessing Multiracial Identity Theory and Politics: The Challenge of Hypodescent," *Ethnicities* 4, no. 3 (2004).

4. I acknowledge that individuals and even groups may lay claim to earlier initiatives in support of a federal multiracial category. Nonetheless, such earlier efforts did not match the scope and publicity of those that began to coalesce in the early 1990s.

5. The activist element has slipped from view in part because news stories on multiracial identity are no longer as fashionable as they were in the mid-1990s. Should the popular media once again take up that level of interest in the subject, activists for multiracial identity will no doubt find ready outlets for the expression of their views.

6. Jill Olumide, *Raiding the Gene Pool: The Social Construction of Mixed Race* (London: Pluto, 2002), 174.

7. Laurie M. Mengel, "Triples—The Social Evolution of a Multiracial Panethnicity: An Asian American Perspective," in *Rethinking "Mixed Race,"* eds. David Parker and Miri Song (London: Pluto, 2001), 106.

8. Maria P. P. Root, ed., *Racially Mixed People in America* (Newbury Park, CA: Sage, 1992); Maria P. P. Root, ed., *The Multiracial Experience: Racial Borders as the New Frontier* (Thousand Oaks, CA: Sage, 1996); Naomi Zack, ed., *American Mixed Race: The Culture of Microdiversity* (Lanham: Rowman and Littlefield, 1995).

I

Projection as Reality: Three Authors, Three Studies, One Problem

It seemed that this poor ignorant Monarch—as he called himself—was persuaded that the Straight Line which he called his kingdom, and in which he passed his existence, constituted the whole of the world, and indeed the whole of Space. Not being able either to move or to see, save in his Straight Line, he had no conception of anything out of it.
—Edwin Abbott, *Flatland*[1]

I want to begin this book by examining a trio of recent scholarly monographs on multiracial identity. These texts stand out for several reasons: they are single-authored scholarly books, they are written by self-identified white women, they are interview studies focusing either wholly or in large measure on black/white multiracials, and they present arguments for the adoption of multiracial identity. The books to which I am referring are *The Interracial Experience: Growing Up Black/White Racially Mixed in the United States* (2001), by Ursula Brown; *Claiming Place: Biracial Young Adults of the Post–Civil Rights Era* (2001), by Marion Kilson; and *From Black to Biracial: Transforming Racial Identity Among Americans* (1999), by Kathleen Korgen.[2] Brown's book and Kilson's book are focused exclusively on black/white persons, while in Kilson's study approximately 70 percent of the participants are of black/white parentage.[3] I think it is important to assess the reasons why these authors wrote their texts, as well as the intellectual and professional expertise they display in their respective endeavors. The first part of my concern will be addressed in this chapter, while the second part (and as it applies to other work by other authors) will be the subject of continuing analysis in this chapter and throughout the remainder of the book.

Following are the rationales given by these three authors as to why they wrote their texts. Brown writes that her "interest in interracial people originates from two experiences. The first and most important one, perhaps, is being the white partner in a racially mixed marriage and having raised two interracial children. In the process of parenting my children, it became quite apparent to me that for their psychosocial adjustment and self-esteem, meeting the love and nurturing needs they had in common with all children was not enough. Their interracial heritage created unique challenges."[4] Kilson identifies herself as "a professional European American woman . . . my husband is African American and my children are Biracial."[5] Finally, Korgen, under a section heading titled "Why Is a White Woman Interested in Biracial Americans?" offers the following: "My brother's marriage to a black woman strengthened my distaste for disapprovers. . . . This book grew out of my desire to understand what life will be like for my nephew as a biracial American."[6]

While there are indeed relatively many more single-authored scholarly books on multiracial identity available today as opposed to in the recent past, the total number is still only a handful. Therefore these three texts represent a significant portion of that recent, single-authored scholarship, and as such I am concerned deeply by what I see as an almost trivial entrée into the field by academics who may well have no business being there. As we shall see, there are significant similarities between these three authors and nonscholar white mothers of black/white multiracial children in general—differences that one would expect scholarly training and intellectual objectivity to have served as a guard against.

Anticipating initial reaction to the foregoing expression of concern, I want to be as explicit as possible in stating that I am in no way suggesting that only multiracial people should write books on multiracial identity, or that white women in particular should not write such books. I welcome intelligent, well-researched, and philosophically sound texts regardless of the writer's background and regardless of the writer's positions on the issues. At the same time, I refuse in the strongest terms to engage in the uncritical acceptance of scholarly books whose primary claim to legitimacy is that their white authors have multiracial children, nieces, or nephews whom they desire to "understand" and "help." The determining justification should be professional or academic expertise, not some notion of personal or emotional authenticity. In other words, we should listen to what Brown, Kilson, and Korgen have to say only if they have well-articulated and persuasively argued points to make, not simply because they are white, women academics who decided to write books on multiracial identity as a result of having multiracial relatives and who found publishers willing to print those books.

Jill Olumide links multiracial activism by whites to antiracist activism by whites, seeing them both as activities that may take on lives of their own quite apart from the needs and goals of the communities supposedly being served: "This is particularly relevant to the 'ought' claims made about a mixed race identity both in areas of welfare work and in some forms of psychology. On whose behalf and with whose authority are these people actually speaking? Is this more a strategy for claiming professional expertise than a genuine desire to address issues of race in the lives of their clientele?"[7] To Olumide's concern I would add the problem of white academics as parents losing any sense of real objectivity while engaging in the kind of personal crusade I made reference to in the book's introduction.

Having made this general point, it would do well to continue by defining in an explicit way the subject matter under consideration before us, namely multiracial identity. What does it mean to be multiracial, to express a multiracial identity? What, precisely, is being conveyed by someone who makes the claim that she or he is multiracial, or that she or he is the parent of a multiracial child? The very first thing it means is that expressers of this identity, or advocates who argue in support of its expression, believe in, accept, and endorse the concept of biological race. We must from the very beginning, and with no equivocation whatsoever, understand that this is an absolutely necessary and sufficient condition for the expression of multiracial advocacy on any level. Multiracial people can come into being only via the sexual reproduction of two progenitors of different biological races. To assert that one is multiracial is to assert that one is the biological child or the further-removed biological descendant of two persons of different racial groups. In either case, persons of different biological races, as a result of sexual procreation, have produced the multiracial person.

David Parker and Miri Song provide the following explanation of multiracial identity, an explanation that ties it firmly to notions of biological race: "To identify someone as 'multiracial' is to enumerate a genealogy that combines a number of distinct 'races' which that person now embodies. It merely displaces the monoracial designation to a higher branch of the family tree. This reinscribes the notion of multiraciality within the discourse of mono-racialisation."[8] Given that I write from the metatheoretical perspective as opposed to the advocacy perspective, I am especially in agreement with Steven Ropp's goal of distinguishing "between discourses which simply reinscribe race upon multiracial subjects and the counter-discourses that might actually challenge racial thinking, racial formations, and racism."[9] One such distinction is recognizing that to assert that one is multiracial, or that one's children are multiracial, but that one does not believe in biological race as a physical reality, is, very simply, to espouse nonsense.

To be sure, proidentity academics for the most part recognize this difficulty and endeavor to evade it through talk of race as a "social construction" or as "socially defined," but such maneuvers are ineffective. Actually, I should be more precise in stating that these maneuvers are ineffective logically, but not necessarily ineffective in general. By this I mean that while the a priori reality is that appeals to race as a social designation as opposed to a biological designation are groundless epistemologically, the maneuver seems to nonetheless work, if the number of authors who make use of the practice and if the relative silence of opposition to it are any indication. Here again is the point of this book—to demand scholarly accountability for the proidentity assertions made under the heading of multiracial identity studies.

What do I mean in referring to such evasive maneuvers? They generally tend to fall to one or the other of at least two types, so let us review an example of each. Kilson provides what I term the "typical sociological confession" when she informs us that "among social scientists today, 'race' is regarded as a social construct. However, as Mukhopadhyay and Moses recently have observed, '[R]aces, though social constructions, do have a material reality and are in some sense and in some context biological groupings.'"[10] In other words, after paying insincere homage to the scientific truth, Kilson, in characteristic sociologist fashion, then proceeds to take her seat at the banquet table of biological race. This is a common practice among sociologists and is especially prevalent in the discourse on multiracial identity, where the inconvenient reality of race's falsehood must be dispensed with at the surface level before the author can progress to a discussion that in fact treats race no differently than what one would expect to find in the pages of a pseudoscientific paper of two hundred years ago. By taking this approach, authors such as Kilson can—always in the first few pages—state that of course biological race is a fallacy and then with complete impunity charge ahead and invoke that fallacy over and over again as a "material reality."

The second evasive approach does not involve an outright bait-and-switch with biological race as does the first, but instead attempts to dispense with biological race altogether by appealing to "socially defined" race, as Maria Root does when she states that today's multiracial young people "come of age when race is defined less by biology than by social construction."[11] Of course, what is left unsaid is that there is absolutely no difference between the old racial paradigm once defined by biology and the new racial paradigm embraced now as a social construction. It is precisely the same paradigm under a different name.

Brown provides an additional example of this second usage in her explanation that the term *interracial* refers to "the biological child of one socially defined black and one socially defined white parent."[12] The goal of this maneuver, of course, is to avoid the conundrum and difficulties inherent in biological race by ignoring the problem altogether. Yet precisely how does the invocation of race as socially defined make any difference at all? This is an argument I have been making for more than seven years, and it has yet to be engaged in a direct way by even one pro–multiracial identity scholar.[13] The challenge I issued years ago, which still stands unanswered, is this: How can the socially defined races of parents be an acceptable criterion for categorizing the *biological* children of those parents? It is not sufficient to merely state that one is invoking socially defined race, as convenient a tactic as that might be. The same means for categorizing the parents should be utilized in categorizing the children. Anything else would represent the height of inconsistency. The recognition of so basic a fact as this is what ought to separate the academic work of scholars from the emotionally charged pleadings of nonscholar activists.

G. Reginald Daniel is another academic who employs the legerdemain of socially designated race in his explanation: "'first-generation' individuals have one parent who is both socially and self-designated as black and one who is socially and self-designated as white, regardless of these parents' actual racial genealogy."[14] Let us for the moment accept the idea of categorizing people via their socially defined race. In doing so we may posit a set of parents, one of whom is socially defined as black and one of whom is socially defined as white. How shall we categorize their biological child? To be consistent we should therefore again appeal to socially defined race; and if we did so, of course, the child would most likely be categorized as black via the social mechanism of hypodescent.[15] Yet proidentity scholars such as Brown and Daniel would have us categorize the parents on the basis of socially defined race, but categorize the resultant child biologically, which merely and inconsistently displaces the problem of biological race from one level to another. Clearly this maneuver is intended to evade the problem of biological race, but just as clear is the fact that the attempted evasion is a bankrupt one. There simply is no logical justification for categorizing the parents one way but categorizing their child another.

Korgen also makes use of the evasive maneuver of socially defined race in her arguments supporting multiracial identity. Relying on the "marginal person" theory propounded by Robert Park and Everett Stonequist (such reliance being a problem in itself, but one that must be bypassed in the present discussion), Korgen writes that "marginality, like race, is socially defined. Just as race is socially determined, so are marginal persons."[16] But if race is socially determined and not biological, why then are black/white multiracials not black in Korgen's view? If race is socially determined as Korgen tells us, then on the basis of her own argument persons of black/white heritage should accept the socially determined black racial designation assigned them by society in the United States. Were Korgen to evidence minimal logical consistency with her own argument, she would be forced to conclude that a social determination of her nephew as black is correct, and that talk of multiracial identity in his case is inappropriate.

The foregoing examples illustrate the very serious problem I am highlighting in this book. If proidentity academics demonstrated a requisite measure of logical consistency, there would be no need for corrective polemics in support of salvaging the intellectual future of the field of multiracial identity studies. It is a problem that allows Brown to write, in regard to one of three interview subjects whose data she decided to remove from her study, that "the third looked interracial but had two socially defined black parents."[17] Wrapped up in this brief statement are enough confusion and inconsistency to call into question the study itself. What does it mean to *look* interracial? Who *looks* interracial and who does not? Would Brown say that most Afro-Americans *look* interracial?[18] Would it matter if one of the "two socially defined black parents" actually *looked* white but was known to have sub-Saharan African ancestry, thereby leading to the black social definition? As I try for a moment to capture in my mind the utter endlessness of phenotypes that are the result of sub-Saharan African and European population-mixing over the past nearly four hundred years, I am reminded of a complaint made by a person interviewed by Olumide: "You certainly couldn't go to town and buy a picture of a mixed race child."[19] One wonders precisely what kind of *look* it is that Olumide's informant and Brown are seeking.

All three of the highlighted authors—Brown, Kilson, and Korgen—opted to use the "snowball" technique as a means of finding multiracial interview subjects for their interview studies. This technique involves obtaining research subjects in a word-of-mouth manner from one person to another. For example, a person the researcher has interviewed might make available the names of additional persons the researcher might be interested in contacting. The advantage of the snowball method is that if one can find a few interview subjects, there is the possibility that those few persons may know of others who share whatever characteristic it is the researcher is focusing on. The disadvantage of the snowball method, especially if it is used as the primary or exclusive means of garnering research subjects, is that the use of personal associations in this manner is likely to lead to a nondiverse study sample. In particular, persons who are thus recommended are likely to be in the same social class as the recommender, thereby resulting in an unrepresentative sample unless one is actually looking only for interview subjects of a certain social class. I do understand these authors' claims regarding the difficulty of finding research subjects, a difficulty that led each of them to rely on snowballing; but I nonetheless question that reliance.

It seems to me that one of three alternatives should be employed in these situations. The first alternative is to roll up one's sleeves and truly do the work of going out and finding a representative sample of research subjects. It may indeed be inconvenient if one cannot find them via notices posted at elite college campuses and coffee houses, but real people may be found in other places as well. The second alternative is to simply not conduct any interviews if one cannot establish a representative sample. Sometimes one must accept the fact that the data one would like to have are just not obtainable at the present time, as opposed to manipulating the data one *can* find to accord conveniently with one's preconceived conclusions. The third alternative is to proceed with conducting skewed research if one feels one absolutely must, to describe it clearly as such, and to not under any conditions attempt to generalize that skewed research to the broader population of multiracial Americans or to any subset of them other than one's unrepresentative research sample.

The three authors differ in the approaches they took. Brown can for the most part be said to have taken the latter alternative, with an important caveat that I shall address below. While she did rely on the snowball method, which led to her research sample being unrepresentative, she did nonetheless provide some qualification of her findings. Neither Kilson nor Korgen opted for any of the alternatives, however. Each instead took the snowballing route, obtained wildly unrepresentative samples as a consequence (I will provide more particulars on that presently), and proceeded to generalize those findings by arguing that their wholly unrepresentative samples actually were representative of some *new* generation of multiracial people. I realize that my assertions concerning the sloppiness of the work of these and other academics writing from the advocacy position may raise some eyebrows, but I stand firmly on those statements and invite anyone to justify the scholarly legitimacy of the material I am here about to critique.

To begin with, each of the three authors acknowledges relying on the snowball method of acquiring interview subjects. Kilson "used 'snowball' sampling to find project participants."[20] For Brown it "was a word of mouth referral process or the 'snowball' method that finally proved most effective in finding potential candidates for this project."[21] Finally, Korgen relates that "a combination of ads in college newspapers, personal contacts, and the snowball effect enabled me to fill my sampling goal of interviewees rather quickly and easily."[22] Let me state clearly that I am not criticizing the snowball method in general, as in certain circumstances it may well be perfectly appropriate. What I am criticizing in the present context is the use of the snowball method in combination with not only a failure to acknowledge the corresponding limitations of the subsequent results, but also an attempt to actually misrepresent those unrepresentative results as more broadly generalizable data. This, as with other criticisms I shall levy, is a heavy charge. The ensuing discussion will substantiate it.

As I indicated above, I view Brown's research design somewhat differently than that of either Kilson or Korgen. In general, I would place Brown's work at least one or possibly several tiers higher than the work of the other two, even though Brown did use the snowball method and did thereby amass an unrepresentative sample. Precisely because of a heavy reliance on the snowball method, Brown ended up with a research sample—as did Kilson and Korgen—that was highly unrepresentative in terms of education, region, and social class. Brown included the results of 119 subjects in her study. Most of these interviewees were students, many of whom "attended prestigious and private universities such as Harvard, Yale, Princeton, Columbia, Wesleyan, and Tufts."[23] Also included in the study were students from "smaller private schools" such as "Bucknell and Lock Haven Universities and Marymount-Manhattan and Middlebury colleges."[24] Indeed, of Brown's 119 interview subjects, only 16 were from "state and city universities such as Rutgers, Hunter College, and City University of New York."[25]

However, to Brown's credit she provides a qualification by stating that "because many of the study respondents came from middle-class backgrounds, the sample was biased and not necessarily representative of the population at large."[26] As we shall see directly, Kilson offers a minimal qualification; however, for lack of a better term, Kilson's is not a *sincere* qualification. Brown's is relatively more sincere because she strives generally throughout her book to consistently use phrases such as "the majority of the participants," or "the men and women who participated in this nonclinical study," without the overt generalization of her results to a broader population.[27] One might well ask if this is not simply the commonsense professionalism we should expect of an academic author, but as we shall see below neither Kilson nor Korgen display the slightest qualms about referring to their particular interview subjects on the one hand, and broader populations of young multiracials on the other, in a completely interchangeable way.

This is not to say that I do not find serious problems in Brown's work, for I do. However, the majority of those problems fall more appropriately to the chapters that follow. Yet even though I have praised Brown—relatively speaking at least, in regard to Kilson and Korgen—for her general forthrightness in not overgeneralizing her research, there are points to be made here as well. The title of Brown's book, *The Interracial Experience,* is troubling because of the word "The." Some will no doubt consider this to be a relentless and overly extensive criticism on my part, but it is vital to understand and acknowledge that there is *no* singular interracial experience any more than there is any singular Afro-American or any singular Euro-American experience. Yet such a singular experience is precisely what is implied by a title such as *The Interracial Experience.* Moreover, if we examine the subtitle we will find that my criticism is upheld, for *Growing Up Black/White Racially Mixed in the United States*—with no mention of the educational, regional, and social class limitations that Brown herself admits to—represents, as does the main title, a suggestion that the study speaks from a much broader perspective than it actually does.

At a very minimum—and recognizing that it would still not be as accurate as it should be—a subtitle such as "Growing Up Black/White Racially Mixed *and Middle-Class* in the United States" would nonetheless have been far more accurate than the subtitle Brown eventually chose. Let me state as well that I am aware of the potential influence of a publisher in the selection of a book's eventual title. However, even acknowledging this influence, there is nonetheless no justification for an academic author either choosing or accepting a title that is false, misleading, or otherwise inaccurate.

Additionally, although Brown does not generalize her findings overtly, she nonetheless offers normative advice for parents of multiracial children throughout her text—normative advice that derives clearly from her "not necessarily representative" findings. So there is still a sense in which Brown's reliance on snowballing results in overgeneralization, but as we shall see in considering the work of Korgen and Kilson, Brown's is a minor version of the problem, relatively speaking.

Korgen interviewed forty biracial adults for her study.[28] In her words, "by most accounts, forty appears to be a good number of interviews to include in a study such as this."[29] Thirty-two of these interviewees were under age thirty, and eight were over that age.[30] Given the fact that Korgen's goal was to compare the experiences and racial identity choices of black/white Americans born before and after 1965, it is perfectly reasonable to criticize her four-to-one ratio as making for a remarkably skewed sample. Her explanation is that "finding biracial persons over the age of thirty was much more difficult. Not only is the population relatively small, it is almost impossible to locate. I did not want to rely on the few interracial organizations that exist because I was seeking a more representative sample of older black-white Americans."[31]

Finding a representative sample of *younger* black/white Americans was apparently of little concern to Korgen, however, since "young adults who are students at (or who have recently graduated from) Boston-area colleges comprised the majority of the subsample of biracial persons born after 1965."[32] Indeed, Korgen's use of the terms "majority" and "subsample" in the previous sentence grossly understates the extent of unrepresentativeness, as in fact "all but two persons in this sample attend or recently graduated from college."[33] Yet amazingly, in my view, Korgen rationalizes away this significant lack of representativeness by suggesting that the broader population of young black/white multiracials must surely be the most highly educated segment of the US population: "My experience finding interviewees reflects the changing demographics of the biracial population."[34] What we see here are serious irregularities and problems at the foundational stages of research project design. Yet as damaging as Korgen's structural problems are, they pale in comparison to those of Kilson.

Kilson describes her decision to use the snowball method as follows: "Given the sensitivity of my research inquiry, I consider the 'snowball' method of finding project participants not only appropriate but probably essential. Nevertheless, I recognize that the method may have led to regional, socioeconomic, and racial bias in my interview sample."[35] Once having made this qualification, however, these important biases are then forgotten most promptly. It should be clear by now that such a nominal attempt to move quickly beyond the problem is simply not adequate, as convenience cannot be allowed to trump research integrity. Of course, some bias is unavoidable, and I would not be so stringent as to suggest that any bias at all is grounds for the strong criticisms I am here levying. It will be best to allow Kilson's own words to catalog the biases stemming from the design of her study but that she nonetheless accepted. This will be a selected listing of the major examples of unrepresentativeness, as it would take up far too much space to list them all. I want to highlight as well the fact that this hugely unrepresentative research sample comprises only fifty-two individuals, which serves to exaggerate the problem even more.

Kilson's fifty-two interviewees included "nine sets of siblings and four sets of spouses."[36] Moreover, "twenty of the fifty-two interviewees had at least one sibling who also participated in the project."[37] In terms of regional diversity, "at the time of the interviews, 16 (31%) lived in Massachusetts, 3 in Connecticut, 16 in the Mid-Atlantic, 7 in the Midwest, and 10 in the West."[38] Of the interviewees' parents, "all fathers had completed high school and all but two mothers, who were born in Asia, had as well. Thirty-seven mothers and thirty-five fathers had graduated from college, while twenty-five fathers and nine mothers held doctorates."[39] Finally, the educational attainment of the interviewees themselves serves to illustrate how very wildly unrepresentative Kilson's research sample is, as "at the time of the interviews, six held doctorates, ten a master's degree or post-master's certificate, twenty-six a baccalaureate degree, six had had some college or technical college experience, and the remainder had completed high school. Thus, the project participants were well-educated young adults with middle- or upper middle-class occupational aspirations and achievements."[40]

What is perhaps most amazing here—more astounding even than the skewed sample itself—is Kilson's utter unwillingness to question it. Instead, like Korgen, she simply rationalizes away this huge problem by stating that "although most of the project participants hold middle- and upper middle-class occupational positions, their socioeconomic status corresponds to that of their generation of Biracial Americans," thereby effectively nullifying her already weak admission, made only one page earlier, that reliance on the snowball method "may have led" to bias in her study.[41] Yet surely her claim of socioeconomic correspondence is sheer nonsense of the utmost circularity. We have been provided with no evidence for believing that Kilson's research sample is in any way representative of "their generation of Biracial Americans" or of any particular generation of biracial Americans. Kilson reports that her book "seeks to understand the personal social constructs of multiracial Americans," yet how can she do this with any intellectual validity if her research sample is so obviously and so profoundly unrepresentative?[42] Kilson claims that her book "differs from previous books on Biracial American young adults in that it seeks to present an ethnographic overview of major issues in the lives of a diverse set of Biracial Americans of the post–Civil Rights generation."[43] But there is not even the pretense of diversity here, except in comments such as the foregoing, which are at a complete variance with the facts of her research sample itself.

It is imperative that scholars who care about the field of multiracial identity studies and its integrity step up and declare finally and firmly that enough is enough. If academics such as Korgen and Kilson want to argue that some new generation of multiracial Americans matches the profiles of their highly skewed research samples, they need to go out and prove it by some means other than referring back in circular fashion to the mere two handfuls (forty for Korgen and fifty-two for Kilson) of affluent, college-educated people they themselves interviewed. Brown at least, excepting the deceptive title and subtitle of her text, does not engage in this brand of overt and unjustified generalization.

Additionally, I have in another place seen what Kilson and Korgen are doing. It calls to mind the work of Edward Reuter in his book *The Mulatto in the United States* (1918), in which he strove to show that mulattoes were superior to blacks and were the natural leaders of a permanent black underclass.[44] I hear a few echoes of this in the work of Kilson and Korgen, who go out of their way via flagrantly flawed research to construct their own vision of young adult black/white Americans as representing a superior type. I want to be clear that I am not suggesting that these two authors in any way share Reuter's generally racist views, but I do question whether Kilson and Korgen are consciously or unconsciously displaying a bias toward their own children · and nephew, respectively, in their work. Kilson in particular seems to all but gush in describing the educational attainments of her interviewees and their parents, which can very easily be seen as a projected and positive reflection of her own children and herself.

Although the questionable foundations of these authors' research designs are clear, I think it necessary to illustrate as well how those questionable foundations—when generalized illegitimately—are utilized to manufacture equally questionable conclusions that are then propounded as if they were in fact valid. For example, even though Korgen's interview sample consists of a highly unrepresentative grouping, she nonetheless consistently generalizes her results to a far broader population: "Like members of any marginal group, biracial men and women possess a broader and more objective view of society than non-marginal persons. Those who claim a biracial identity view race and our race-based society in general in a markedly different manner than the average monoracial American. The vast majority of the under-thirty interviewees agree with Park that they are more 'cosmopolitan' than non-mixed persons."[45] Beyond the likelihood that most people who attend or have graduated from college, if asked whether they are more cosmopolitan than some other "ordinary" group would probably respond that they indeed are, we must keep in mind that Korgen is referring to the "vast majority" of a mere thirty-two, highly unrepresentative individuals; yet she offers absolutely no qualification of her results.

Similarly, when making another clear and unambiguous claim about the younger generation of black/white Americans, Korgen does so without in any way qualifying this particular claim: "As the case studies in Chapter 2 illustrate, biracial persons born after the Civil Rights Movement are much more likely to identify as biracial than are those born before the Movement. A full two-thirds of this younger cohort feel free to recognize both sides of their racial heritage."[46] Yet again, she is referring to a "full two-thirds" of an unrepresentative thirty-two individuals and then unjustifiably generalizing that result to a much broader population. Moreover, in reading *From Black to Biracial,* the reader does not become aware of the full extent of the unrepresentativeness and paucity of Korgen's interview sample until an appendix on methodology just prior to the bibliography. Instead, the reader is led to believe that Korgen's unqualified generalizations are legitimate. Less careful readers and readers who skip the appendix altogether will never realize the invalidity of what they have read, assuming instead that they have been engaging actual research.

Thus, when Korgen declares that "while the majority of such persons [black/white Americans] born immediately prior to the Movement perceive themselves as black, most young adult offspring of black/white couples define themselves as biracial," nothing is revealed at that point concerning the flawed nature of the research sample.[47] Likewise, when Korgen announces that, "as illustrated by these case studies, there has been a transformation in how biracial persons racially identify themselves. Biracial adults raised after the Civil Rights era are much less likely to consider themselves to be black than are mixed-race persons over the age of thirty," the reader does not yet know that this major conclusion is based on a woefully unrepresentative sample of "case studies" numbering thirty-two and eight.[48]

Kilson's illegitimately generalized statements are of the same type, and although she divulges her highly skewed interview sample early on (as I have noted, she rationalizes it effusively to accommodate her own particular projection), she consistently and continuously generalizes her results in a manner that is simply unacceptable in the realm of scholarly discourse. Given what we know about her interview sample, the following assertion is simply false: "Although most Biracial Americans (54%) stated that they would prefer to live in a racially and ethnically diverse community, this preference was stronger among women (59%) than men (44%)."[49] As we know, "most" biracial Americans stated no such thing; rather, 54 percent of her fifty-two unrepresentative individuals did. Consider as well the following declaration by Kilson: "As these selections suggest, for most Biracial Americans, racial identity evolves and changes over time. Today most of the Biracial young adults with whom I spoke . . ."[50] My immediate reaction to the preceding is to question whether Kilson is referring to "most Biracial Americans" or to "most of the Biracial young adults with whom [she] spoke," for the two groups are clearly not synonymous.

All three of these authors relied on snowball sampling, resulting in highly skewed research data that they, to varying degrees, represent as embodying the characteristics of the broader young multiracial (or specifically black/white) population of the United States today. For the most part, Brown's study does this through its title and subtitle, and via her normative statements throughout the text. Although some might object that I am unduly critical of Brown on this point, I stand firm in my assertion that her title and subtitle are in fact key pathways for misrepresentation or misunderstanding to occur. When one picks up Brown's book, when one refers to it in scholarly writing, and when one includes it in bibliographies, the generalizing effect of the words "The Interracial Experience" and "Growing Up Black/White Racially Mixed in the United States" is significant. When one encounters the latter set, one is not thinking of research based predominantly on middle-class students at prestigious, private, northeastern universities. So I maintain that Brown's title and subtitle are illegitimate generalizations, regardless of the relatively ungeneralizing nature of her text itself.

As scholarly research on multiracial identity studies, Kilson's book is simply inadequate; as scholarly research on multiracial identity studies, Korgen's book is simply inadequate. If no one else is willing to state these important facts due to politeness or for whatever reason, I do so here and now. As in the case of Brown, their respective titles and subtitles (*Claiming Place: Biracial Young Adults of the Post–Civil Rights Era,* and *From Black to Biracial: Transforming Racial Identity Among Americans*) are gross and unjustified overgeneralizations; but unlike in the case of Brown at least, the actual content of both Kilson's text and Korgen's text abounds consistently in repeated overgeneralizations from beginning to end without appropriate acknowledgment that the two authors' research subject pools are outrageously unrepresentative of the populations they are so invalidly generalizing to. I find it difficult to emphasize strongly enough that the conclusions Kilson and Korgen propound in regard to young, multiracial Americans are completely unsubstantiated and wholly invalid. If one wants to know what is wrong today with the quality of advocacy scholarship, here are two prime examples.

During the 1990s it was not uncommon for proidentity activists and white mothers to confuse the difference between race and culture in their arguments for a federal multiracial category. This was surely to be expected, as these people were neither academics nor intellectuals of any sort. Today, though, it is surprising and somewhat disappointing to discover proidentity academics continuing to follow suit. Earlier in this chapter I addressed the conflating of biological race and social race by these academics, but in addition to this we find a conflating of race and culture in the proidentity academic literature. However, whereas in the former case the conflating is a purposeful attempt to avoid the messy fact that advocacy of multiracial identity requires a corresponding belief in biological race, the latter phenomenon seems to be more a case of simple scholarly sloppiness and factual error.

For instance, Brown notes that many in her subject pool "were raised in predominantly white or racially integrated communities where white culture was an integral part of life," and that "the more interracial children were immersed in white cultural life, the more they identified with it."[51] It is not altogether clear that this conclusion has anything in particular to do with interracial children, however. Indeed, if we are addressing manifestations of behavior that one might *popularly* categorize as racial, many are the cases of Afro-American children who have grown up in predominantly white environments and who have essentially manifested what the general public would consider to be white identities. This, after all, is the source of that derogatory term "oreo," which refers to someone considered black on the outside but white on the inside, regardless of the person's phenotype.[52] The same phenomenon may be said to hold in the reverse case, although it is likely a significantly rarer occurrence.

So this is not to say that Brown's conclusion is incorrect, but rather to point out that it is likely irrelevant. Any person acculturated to a particular environment, especially at a young age, is going be impacted significantly by that experience. As Tanya Hernández describes, the proponents of federally recognized multiracial identity misconstrue race "as solely a cultural identification. Specifically, such a demand presupposes that there are 'pure-Black' experiences, which make a person authentically Black, and inversely, that the lack of such authenticating experiences makes a person 'less Black.'"[53] The error Hernández points out is mirrored in Brown's overly simplistic view of race and culture.

We may be sure that we have not been in error in concluding that Brown conflates race and culture, for she again makes this confusion plain when she writes that "interracial children may experience this clash of cultures particularly intensely, since they harbor both black and white racial heritages within themselves."[54] Yet precisely what does "harboring" a racial heritage mean, and how is it related to culture? Is it a form of genetic imprinting, something that operates of its own accord in a racially stereotypical way? Brown would by her assertion appear to be suggesting nothing less—and in an important sense nothing more—than the old pathology trope of the tragic mulatto (see Chapter 2), in which black/white persons are supposedly in a perpetual emotional war with themselves. I insist on interrogating these kinds of assertions in an aggressive way because they are seriously dubious statements, and should not be suffered to become part of the discourse without challenge.

I will admit to experiencing an odd sort of bemusement when I read Brown, the white female academic, instructing me—a person with a self-identified white mother and a self-identified black father—as to the particularly intense clash of cultures I should experience due to my harbored racial heritages. But then I think of the damage her assertion does to the scholarly integrity of multiracial identity studies, and it is no longer amusing. Do I harbor two racial heritages within me? If so, I certainly cannot feel them, evaluate them, or otherwise gain access to them now, nor could I when I was a child. I can also state honestly that I have never experienced a "clash of cultures" of any kind, whether intensely or mildly.

I find it impossible here to take Brown as a serious scholar and at the same time understand what she intends by referring to people harboring "both black and white racial heritages within themselves." One thinks of a psychological time bomb waiting to go off, perhaps. We might imagine a black/white infant who is adopted by two Afro-

American parents. Will her harbored racial heritages begin intense war-fare within her as her adoptive parents stand silently by, knowing what is happening but helpless to stop it? Or will the harbored racial heritages only go to battle with each other if the child discovers somehow that she is racially mixed? Even if some intellectual (or biological) sense could be made of the notion of people harboring both black and white racial heritages within themselves, what would it have to do with culture any-way?

"Heritage" is a term that, especially as applied to race, is overused and exaggerated. As Ropp notes in a somewhat sarcastic vein: "Beyond being 'culturally' American and 'biologically' biracial, I cannot figure out how to access those German and Japanese heritages that people keep talking about."[55] The bottom line is that I have no racial heritage, nor does anyone else. There are indeed histories that some people share, but even those histories are not shared equally by the members of any par-ticular group or groups, and are instead more like an unending series of partially overlapping sets in a Venn diagram. Indeed, I might even go so far as to venture that the notion of a personal heritage—a family her-itage, for instance—is a questionable one, but delving into that would take us too far afield from the subject at hand.

Other authors writing in support of multiracial identity also conflate race and culture. For instance, Kilson gives this description: "These young adult Biracial Americans, like others with whom I spoke, value not only their ability to move comfortably within and between cultures but their insights into different cultural worlds, which they perceive derive from their multicultural experiences as Biracial Americans."[56] Yet is Kilson referring here to biracialism or biculturalism, and is there any difference between the two? Indeed, does presumed race even mat-ter to cultural insight? It seems to me that we are operating at an extremely low level of intellectual analysis if we accept such assertions without critical challenge. As mentioned above, people may become acclimated to different cultural styles regardless of their supposed race. In fact, a fundamental point assumed by these writers, but that cries out for interrogation, is the question of whether whiteness and blackness—to take one often-invoked presumption—truly represent two separate cultures in the United States in the first place.

I realize that for some this may be a fantastic question, a query whose affirmative answer is patently obvious. However, the obviousness of an affirmative response is not at all apparent to me. Mary Texeira makes the important observation that "some multiracialists also argue that unless they embrace this [multiracial] category they are rejecting their white parent's culture, ignoring the fact that European Americans and African Americans have cultures that are so blended as to be, at times, indistinguishable."[57] What is often appealed to (unknowingly, apparently) when proidentity academics craft this dual-culture supposition is neither a racial nor a cultural distinction, but rather a class distinction. In fact, all three interview studies I am examining in this chapter deal exclusively or very substantially with black/white persons who grew up in or have been exposed to generally affluent environments. One does not come across US studies in which representative numbers of the respondents are black/white children reared in inner-city ghettos or in the poverty-stricken conditions of rural Appalachia. Granted, the latter scenario is far less likely than the former, but I am aware of no study offered by advocates of US multiracial identity in which even the former scenario is at all engaged, and I believe there is a reason for this lapse.[58]

Studying the US multiracial identity movement, Kim Williams finds a lack of class diversity among the people who make up that population: "The basic socioeconomic indicators of my respondents, generally speaking, show that people involved in these groups look a lot like mainstream middle-class Americans, if somewhat more affluent."[59] Stephen Small raises a similar point regarding the American multiracial identity movement, noting that it is "dominated by middle-class Americans, largely unreflective about the class basis of their own demands, and one searches in vain to hear what people from working class and poor communities might have to say."[60] It is telling that we find ourselves searching in vain for the same thing in regard to these interview studies. It is almost as if Brown, Kilson, and Korgen each went explicitly in search of people just like their own children and nephew, respectively, to serve as interview subjects for their studies.[61]

A critical point must be made here, one that might possibly be lost if not stated explicitly. I am not denying that the organizations constituting the US multiracial identity movement are made up largely of middle-class people. There is no doubt about that fact, and indeed it is an extremely relevant fact. What I am denying is that one can conduct accurate research and provide legitimate scholarly generalizations on the broader population of multiracial (or specifically black/white) Americans—of any age group—by interviewing only those who are in the middle class and who are therefore much more likely to be active proponents of multiracial identity in the first place. This is the smoke and mirrors behind these studies: the authors purport to generalize about multiracial Americans or about the younger generation of multiracial

Americans, but their research methods selectively target only a particular segment of that population—a segment whose likely leanings in the research matter under consideration poison the very studies themselves. There are very many Americans of black/white and other mixed parentages who are not middle-class and who do not or did not attend elite educational institutions. However, their experiences and their views are not included in these studies because, as the researchers themselves attest, it is too inconvenient to find them.

The far easier path is to employ snowball sampling of multiracial students at a few elite, northeastern colleges and then unjustifiably generalize to all multiracial persons (or to all those of a particular age group) the unrepresentative results one thereby produces. Therefore, returning once again to our discussion of race and culture, Kilson uses her study to suggest that multiracial Americans' encounter with white culture "can be more complex than for monoracial Americans of color, because they often have an intimate connection to the dominant culture that does not fully embrace them."[62] But is this really true? We do not actually know, for precisely how intimate a connection Kilson intends is not revealed; she merely makes the statement without providing support. What is Kilson really claiming about culture and intimacy?

I again raise the challenge that far too much is being allowed here in regard to supposed real differences of culture, especially between whites and Afro-Americans. The question that must be asked is whether Kilson has something to say about all multiracial Americans, about the particular age group she purports to focus on, or only about the small and unrepresentative group she garnered from snowball sampling in a nondiverse environment. Do Kilson's claims about cultural intimacy extend as well to a black/white teenager living in poverty in an Atlanta slum, a teenager who never knew her uneducated and equally poor white father? If so, then we may say that Kilson's argument could possibly be consistent and justified. If not, however, there is no other conclusion to draw than that her argument is—despite the scholarly trappings in which it is presented—wholly unsupported.

Kilson invokes a similar presumption of distinct US racial cultures when she makes mention of part-white multiracial persons who are raised without exposure to "their other socioracial heritage."[63] But again I ask, what is this? What is one's socioracial heritage, whether from one parent or the other? Unchallenged language of this sort permeates advocacy scholarship, leading to faulty conclusions that are similarly unchallenged. Lest there be any doubt, I can certainly imagine what Kilson likely intends by the term "socioracial heritage"—a biological link to a shared racial history with the prefix "socio" thrown in to counterbalance the clear appeal to biological race. I simply dispute that it has any real meaning beyond being yet another attempt to imply (without argument) that there is a distinct black racial culture in the United States, as she does when proffering "African American culture" as one type of "other socioracial heritage."[64]

In Kilson's view, "while all people of color encounter White culture and racism in the United States, the Biracial experience is more complex. Biracial Americans with European American parentage are integrally related both to the dominant culture and to other ethnic cultures."[65] But what is this integral relation to culture, and do these cultures truly exist qua cultures? Kilson states several times that the multiracial experience is "more complex," but why should this be so? It might be different, but why should it be any more or less complex than a monoracial experience? Again, no reason is offered beyond the assertion itself. Moreover, it is difficult to understand the way in which being multiracial causes one necessarily to be related integrally to two cultures (pretending, for the sake of argument only, that there actually are distinct US racial cultures). What would the nature of this integral relation be? Would it be the same if the person were aware of her *racial heritages* as if she were not?

Audrey Smedley casts the light of day on the issue of supposedly separate US racial cultures when she writes that "some advocates of a new 'mixed-race' category have argued that they need this new identity in order to recognize the 'culture' of their white parent. In American ideology, a black parent presumably has 'black' culture, and the white parent has 'white' culture, with the unstated understanding that these are incompatible ways of life. Aside from the fact that this idea is nonsense, it continues to feed the psychic stress of a few individuals who have the feeling that they do not know who they are."[66]

There is much more to say regarding the flaws of this trio of interview studies, and I am concerned to make my point with clarity and the requisite force but without belaboring it unnecessarily. It is critical, however, that we understand precisely how the combination of flawed research design, carelessness, personal bias and projection, and the decision to allow the convenience of the snowball method to take precedence over the hard work of real research can lead to published conclusions that are in fact completely unsubstantiated. Not only must we understand this important fact, but we must uncover and reject all instances of the phenomenon whenever it surfaces in the work of academics writing in the field of multiracial identity studies.

Since the emergence of the multiracial identity movement in the early 1990s, scholarly work on multiracial identity studies—particularly from the proidentity standpoint—has been dominated by authors writing from the perspectives of sociology and psychology. As such, these two disciplines have in a significant way shaped the parameters of discourse on multiracial identity up to this point. In Chapter 2, I will consider some of foundational assumptions that sociology and psychology have imparted to the field of multiracial identity studies. This focus will serve to broaden the discussion, and will assist us in assessing whether the contemporary proidentity stance has really changed very much from the nineteenth- and early-twentieth-century formulation of multiracial identity that had at its center a conception of black/white persons as inherently conflicted and tragically pathological.

Notes

1. Edwin Abbott, *Flatland: A Romance of Many Dimensions,* 2nd ed. (London: Seeley, 1884; reprint, New York: Penguin, 1998), 66.

2. Ursula Brown, *The Interracial Experience: Growing Up Black/White Racially Mixed in the United States* (Westport: Praeger, 2001); Marion Kilson, *Claiming Place: Biracial Young Adults of the Post–Civil Rights Era* (Westport: Bergin and Garvey, 2001); Kathleen Korgen, *From Black to Biracial: Transforming Racial Identity Among Americans* (Westport: Praeger, 1999).

3. Kilson, *Claiming Place,* 86–89. In a table listing the racial identities of her participants' parents, Kilson provides information for forty-nine of her fifty-two interviewees. According to the information provided, black/white persons account for 71.4 percent of her study. Even assuming that the three persons whose information is not included are not black/white, the figure for black/white participants only drops to 67.3 percent.

4. Brown, *The Interracial Experience,* 20.

5. Kilson, *Claiming Place,* xi.

6. Korgen, *From Black to Biracial,* 3–4.

7. Jill Olumide, *Raiding the Gene Pool: The Social Construction of Mixed Race* (London: Pluto, 2002), 174.

8. David Parker and Miri Song, "Introduction: Rethinking 'Mixed Race,'" in *Rethinking "Mixed Race,"* eds. David Parker and Miri Song (London: Pluto, 2001), 10.

9. Steven Ropp, "Do Multiracial Subjects Really Challenge Race? Mixed Race Asians in the United States and the Caribbean," in *"Mixed Race" Studies: A Reader,* ed. Jayne O. Ifekwunigwe (London: Routledge, 2004), 264.

10. Kilson, *Claiming Place,* 5.

11. Maria P. P. Root, "Five Mixed-Race Identities: From Relic to Revolution," in *New Faces in a Changing America: Multiracial Identity in the 21st Century,* eds. Loretta Winters and Herman DeBose (Thousand Oaks, CA: Sage, 2003), 4.

12. Brown, *The Interracial Experience,* 11 n. 2.

13. Rainier Spencer, *Spurious Issues: Race and Multiracial Identity Politics in the United States* (Boulder: Westview, 1999), 89–92.

14. G. Reginald Daniel, *More Than Black? Multiracial Identity and the New Racial Order* (Philadelphia: Temple University Press, 2002), 6.

15. Hypodescent, or the "one-drop rule," is the social mechanism that ensures that the offspring of a member of the highest-status racial group and a member of a lower-status racial group assumes the status of the lower member. In the United States, hypodescent is operative primarily in the case of black/white mixture.

16. Korgen, *From Black to Biracial,* 70.

17. Brown, *The Interracial Experience,* 22.

18. I will return to the question of "looks," and to the historical problem underlying comments such as those of Brown, in Chapter 4.

19. Olumide, *Raiding the Gene Pool,* 99.

20. Kilson, *Claiming Place,* 8.

21. Brown, *The Interracial Experience,* 22.

22. Korgen, *From Black to Biracial,* 121.

23. Brown, *The Interracial Experience,* 22.

24. Ibid.

25. Ibid., 22–23.

26. Ibid., 23.

27. Ibid., 86, 109.

28. Korgen, *From Black to Biracial,* 123.

29. Ibid.

30. Ibid., 130.

31. Ibid., 121.

32. Ibid., 125.

33. Ibid.

34. Ibid., 121.

35. Kilson, *Claiming Place,* 8.

36. Ibid., 11.

37. Ibid., 22.

38. Ibid., 13 n. 4.

39. Ibid., 17.

40. Ibid., 12.

41. Ibid., 9.

42. Ibid.

43. Ibid., 7.

44. Edward Reuter, *The Mulatto in the United States: Including a Study of the Rôle of Mixed-Blood Races Throughout the World* (Boston: Richard G. Badger, 1918; reprint, New York: Negro Universities Press, 1969).

45. Korgen, *From Black to Biracial,* 70.

46. Ibid., 39.

47. Ibid., 3.

48. Ibid., 37.

49. Kilson, *Claiming Place,* 61.

50. Ibid., 50–51.

51. Brown, *The Interracial Experience,* 76.

52. Oreos, of course, are cookies consisting of two chocolate wafers on either side of a white, creamy filling.

53. Tanya K. Hernández, "'Multiracial' Discourse: Racial Classifications in an Era of Color-Blind Jurisprudence," *Maryland Law Review* 57, no. 97 (1998): 106.

54. Brown, *The Interracial Experience,* 44.

55. Ropp, "Do Multiracial Subjects Really Challenge Race?" 266.

56. Kilson, *Claiming Place,* 55.

57. Mary Thierry Texeira, "The New Multiracialism: An Affirmation of or an End to Race As We Know It?" in *New Faces in a Changing America,* eds. Winters and DeBose, 28–29.

58. Kendra Wallace's *Relative/Outsider* is based on a far more socioeconomically diverse sample than those of Brown, Kilson, and Korgen; however, all the respondents in her study come from "one public high school and one private university in the San Francisco Bay area." Kendra Wallace, *Relative/Outsider: The Art and Politics of Identity Among Mixed Heritage Students* (Westport: Ablex, 2001), 7.

59. Kim Williams, "Linking the Civil Rights and Multiracial Movements," in *The Politics of Multiracialism: Challenging Racial Thinking,* ed. Heather M. Dalmage (Albany: State University of New York Press, 2004), 91.

60. Stephen Small, "Colour, Culture, and Class: Interrogating Interracial Marriage and People of Mixed Racial Descent in the USA," in *Rethinking "Mixed Race,"* eds. Parker and Song, 126.

61. It is interesting to note that the authors of two British studies of multiracial identity had no problem finding working-class respondents. It is doubtful that the situations in the United States and the United Kingdom are so radically different that working-class multiracials are simply not to be found in the United States. Anne Wilson, *Mixed Race Children: A Study of Identity* (Boston: Allen and Unwin, 1987); Barbara Tizard and Ann Phoenix, *Black, White, or Mixed Race? Race and Racism in the Lives of Young People of Mixed Parentage* (London: Routledge, 1993).

62. Kilson, *Claiming Place,* 67.

63. Ibid., 68.

64. Ibid.

65. Ibid., 74.

66. Audrey Smedley, *Race in North America: Origin and Evolution of a Worldview,* 2nd ed. (Boulder: Westview, 1999), 332.

2

Psychobabble, Socioblather, and the Reinscription of the Pathology Paradigm

Surely a moment's reflection, and a single instance from common life, must convince every one that our whole social system is based upon Regularity, or Equality of Angles. . . . But I am insulting the intelligence of my Readers by accumulating details which must be patent to everyone who enjoys the advantages of a Residence in Spaceland. Obviously the measurements of a single angle would no longer be sufficient under such portentous circumstances; one's whole life would be taken up in feeling or surveying the perimeter of one's acquaintances. Already the difficulties of avoiding a collision in a crowd are enough to tax the sagacity of even a well-educated square; but if no one could calculate the Regularity of a single figure in the company, all would be chaos and confusion, and the slightest panic would cause serious injuries, or—if there happened to be any Women or Soldiers present— perhaps considerable loss of life.

—Edwin Abbott, *Flatland*[1]

Edwin Abbott's brief but wonderful 1884 novel *Flatland* revolves around people's inability to move outside the constraints of their own arrogant and restricted worldviews. The narrator of this delightful tale is at first unwilling to conceive that life could exist other than as it does in his two-dimensional Flatland, a world whose inhabitants are perfectly flat, geometric figures (some possessing dangerously sharp angles) who cannot rise above or see above the surface plane of their existence. However, a dream journey to one-dimensional Lineland, followed by actual contact from a representative of three-dimensional Spaceland as well as a trip there, and finally a brief visit to nondimensional Pointland, show him the error and the limitation of his ways. He then quickly intuits that there must be a fourth dimension and higher dimensions as well, and begins to badger his three-dimensional guide for the details of this advanced knowledge.

While some might expect that an evocation of *Flatland* in the present context would be in support of arguing that we should open our minds to the possibility of multiracial identity, my use of it is far more basic. I draw on it to illustrate that we must open our minds to the reality that race does not exist, and to the reality that multirace does not exist. I see the didactic lesson of *Flatland* as a metaphor for the inability of people today, particularly academics such as certain sociologists and psychologists, to free themselves from the false belief that race is a reality, whether they bow before biological race at the front of the altar or before socially defined race at the rear of the altar. In either case it is the same altar to the same golden calf.

The common-life example Abbott's narrator refers to above concerns the impossible scenario that would result if the inhabitants of Flatland were not regular geometric figures. (A few irregulars exist, but they are either destroyed at birth, corrected surgically when very young, or doomed to lives of complete social ostracism, including having to reside at their places of work and being forbidden to marry.) Because all the figures one might meet in normal social intercourse are regular, an inhabitant of Flatland can infer accurately, either by feeling or through sight, the shape of a fellow inhabitant (and therefore that inhabitant's social class) by inspection of a single angle. This is critical, since these inhabitants cannot rise above the plane to look down and see one another's shapes. However, such necessary deductions would be impossible if, say, a triangle had a parallelogram attached to one of its vertexes, or if an inhabitant were composed of a "triangular front and a polygonal back," either of these possibilities representing a veritable "monster."[2] Nothing less than complete social chaos would be the inevitable result.

Flatland is an extremely humorous book while at the same time serving as a sublimely clever poke at people's arrogance in their ignorance. The lesson is easily transferable to us as well. Due in part to our history and in part to the retrograde work of modern academics who should know better, the United States still finds itself enthralled to the fantasy of race. We believe that everyone has—or must be made to have—a racial identity, whether that identity is a monoracial one or a multiracial one, and whether that identity is a biologically defined one or a socially defined one. In short, we are unwilling to conceive that life could exist other than as it does in our Raceland, a world whose inhabitants are perfectly race-able figures who cannot rise above or see above the surface plane of their racial existence. Our whole social system is based on race; anything else would surely lead to psychological disorder and social chaos.

In Raceland, happily, those of us who are aware of the falseness of its premises have the right and the opportunity to speak out against the fantasy. This is unlike the situation in fictional Flatland, where heresy on the subject of the existence of more than two dimensions might lead to death, or, as in the case of our narrator, lifetime imprisonment. In Raceland, the costs of heresy for the heretic are likely to be no more than continued frustration and irritation—certainly nothing so severe as in Flatland! The debilitating costs to society of maintaining our Raceland fantasy, however (belief in biological race, racism, pervasive structural inequality, differential life chances, acceptance of fallacious arguments for multiracial identity, unnecessary psychological intervention), are much higher.

Just as the operation of social rules in Flatland has an effect on the lives of its inhabitants, so too does the operation of social rules in Raceland have an effect on our lives. In either case a major basis of social organization is in fact a false consciousness, but in either case the effects on the respective inhabitants are nonetheless significant. This is precisely the point at which scholars in Raceland become critical social actors by either working to expose the fallacy or by working to inscribe it all the more deeply. It is the point at which academics can either firmly and constructively point out that people believe erroneously in a false consciousness, or meekly and unconstructively mewl that the false consciousness has become a real thing because people believe in it. The choice as to how we discharge this important responsibility is all ours.

One of the more disturbing (and frustrating and irritating) aspects of academic writing in support of multiracial identity is the deployment of what I call "psychobabble" and "socioblather." Psychobabble in the present context refers to the use of various questionable psychological theories to put forth arguments in favor of multiracial identity. I am certainly not the first to make use of the former term, and am merely appropriating it here for this specific purpose. I have, however, for lack of a better descriptor, coined the latter term as shorthand for a complementary array of propositions utilized by sociologists in ways similar to those of psychologists engaging in psychobabble. Thankfully, being neither a psychologist nor a sociologist, I am beholden neither to Erik Erickson nor to Robert Park and Everett Stonequist, and I can state with utmost happiness and academic freedom that theirs are altars before which I do not bow.[3]

Never challenged seriously, rarely even questioned, often accepted like baby food—psychobabble and socioblather serve as the academic backbone of multiracial identity efforts and of efforts to validate the reality of biological race. Psychobabble, in being concerned primarily with the individual, is the more foundational of the two, and it merges into socioblather when the presumption that persons of black/white parentage must accept a multiracial identity is extended and amplified such that this identity must be accepted by society as well. Psychobabble informs us that persons of black/white parentage will suffer psychological damage if they are not trained to accept a multiracial identity, while socioblather informs us that this multiracial identity must moreover be accepted by the society at large (ideally in the form of a federal multiracial category) so that such persons' inner identity may be validated outwardly by the external society.

In other words, on the one hand a multiracial identity is appropriate for the individual's psychological development, and on the other it is necessary for the same individual's social existence. Of course, neither psychobabble nor socioblather is restricted to the disciplinary boundaries associated with its respective appellation. In other words, a psychologist may engage in socioblather just as readily as a sociologist may engage in psychobabble. This double-edged sword is exemplified in the work of Ursula Brown, Marion Kilson, and Kathleen Korgen, which I discussed in Chapter 1 and will discuss again here. There are other academics as well who are utilizers of psychobabble and socioblather, and I will consider their arguments in this chapter also.

In earlier days, black/white individuals were assumed to be tragically unfulfilled persons, striving hopelessly to escape the blackness that was their destiny by reaching futilely toward the whiteness they could never truly achieve. An entire academic and literary tradition grew in support of this contention, exemplified by Edward Reuter's scholarly 1918 book *The Mulatto in the United States,* and the two film adaptations (1934, 1959) of Fannie Hurst's 1933 novel *Imitation of Life.*[4] Mulattoes tended to be described in scholarly writing, and portrayed in literature, as being twisted and torn between the two opposed races living uneasily inside them—the pathology trope of the tragic mulatto. This is a view that began to be challenged, if only on the surface, in more modern times and became contested further, again on the surface, as the multiracial identity movement started to come into existence in the early 1990s.

However, an ironic thing occurred in regard to the movement and the old pathology trope. Whereas the people supporting black/white multiracial identity railed against the old trope's suggestion that mulattoes were tragically torn, the arguments they put forth for a federal multiracial category tended nonetheless to reinforce that very trope of tragic multiraciality. This new psychology asserted (and still does) that black/white persons are indeed in a torn and pathological state *unless* they are guided toward a "healthy" multiracial identity.[5] Under the old trope, black/white individuals were pathological if they tried to assume a multiracial identity, while under the new trope they are pathological if they do not. Under the old trope, black/white persons were correct if they identified as black and confused if they identified as multiracial; under the new trope, black/white persons are correct if they identify as multiracial and confused if they identify as black. One wonders precisely how much real progress there is to be found in this mere exchange or reversal of tropes, as it seems that black/white individuals are doomed to congenital pathology in some sense or other no matter what.

A foundational problem here that has mystified psychologists, psychotherapists, and sociologists alike is the fact that we are in the first place dealing with a biological fallacy that has been erected into a psychological and sociological house of cards. This is what Jill Olumide refers to when she points out that it is "within the group that putative problems of identity tend to be located rather than in the wider social world where restrictive and inaccurate racialised identities are allocated."[6] A problem that is actually a social fallacy is postulated instead to lie within the individual or the mixed-race group, "as for 'psychological' marking, almost all the recent research has conceptualised and investigated mixed race as a psychological rather than as a social phenomenon. Pathology is thus located in the group rather than in the social structure which employs race as a main axis of division and mixed race as its unnatural adversary."[7]

In other words, if the fallacy of race is accepted and if mixed-race identity troubles are seen as residing within the person or the group, there then is no motivation to do the necessary work of problematizing the overarching social structure that in the first place deploys race as a false marker of biological difference that can then be distilled into the opiate of socially defined race. Nor does merely pointing out that race is a problem of social structure bring us any closer to doing away with the myth, for sociologists generally do not appreciate the difference between recognizing that people wrongly believe in race on the one hand, and treating race as a reality—social or otherwise—on the other. Sociologists notoriously get this wrong, for it is not race that is a social reality, but rather *belief* in race that is a social reality. The difference is fundamental.

It is my view that academics, including sociologists, have a professional obligation to educate and to shine the light of knowledge on the darkness of ignorance, rather than to reify existing false consciousnesses by acquiescing meekly in them. The assertion of race as a social reality represents precisely such an acquiescence. To accept race as a social reality is to reify biological categorizations of race that were debunked long ago, as the racial categories thereby constructed are no different from those biological categories of centuries ago. To understand that *belief* in race is a social reality, however, is to perceive correctly the societal dynamic that is actually occurring.[8]

If one considers seriously what is actually being asserted by pro-movement academics in regard to the new pathology trope, it is quite an astonishing blend of psychobabble and socioblather rolled into one. An individual born of black and white parentage is de facto born with a problem requiring both specific psychological training and the establishment of a federal multiracial category to resolve it satisfactorily. Therefore, this child needs special instruction to teach her that she is multiracial, or else she will be inauthentic to her true self and will not have her identity validated by society, which can itself only really happen if federal recognition is granted to multiracial identity. This is nothing less than an astounding mirror-image of the old pathology trope—no less dangerous and no less wrong, but deployed with far less excuse in this modern day. As Olumide explains, tragic mulatto pathology is very much centered wrongly in the individual, rather than in a flawed social structure.

Brown gives the following brief account of the tragic mulatto story: "Writers, moviemakers, and social scientists at the beginning of this century created a portrait of interracial people as 'lost souls' whose inner turmoil left them psychologically and emotionally maladjusted. This picture was confirmed in the late 1960s when health professionals began to study a few interracial families and their children in mental health clinics and generalized from the findings to the overall population of mixed race families."[9] Precisely what Brown means by the picture being "confirmed" is unclear, however, as she is commenting on the doubly illegitimate generalizing of "a few" clinical study samples to a broader population.[10] My reading of her text here suggests that she means to be taken literally, though, with no sarcasm intended.

Her own study's conclusion regarding this important point is decidedly inconclusive, as she informs us that the "men and women who participated in this nonclinical study suggest that the image of the 'tragic mulatto' is valid for some mixed race people, but not for other [*sic*]."[11] Yet regardless of Brown's descriptive assertion that the tragic mulatto syndrome affects black/white persons on a continuum, and that some of her study participants were conflicted and some were not, her normative language throughout the text—particularly that multiracial children have "special needs" that must be addressed (see below)—suggests clearly that proper practice in her view is to teach persons of black/white parentage that they are in fact multiracial.[12] Indeed, her admission as to the nongeneralizability of her study (see Chapter 1), and her comment regarding the psychological adjustment of black/white persons being arrayed on a continuum, make it difficult to see how Brown can justify making the major normative assertion that, "as interracial children grow up, the parents should encourage them to embrace both parts of their racial heritage, accept evidence of identity fluctuations, and raise them in a racially mixed community."[13] If in Brown's own sample there was significant variance as to how her respondents were situated psychologically in regard to their racial identities, it is then strange that she finds it nonetheless acceptable to offer such a one-size-fits-all solution to so complex a scenario.

Just as Flatland's "whole social system is based upon Regularity, or Equality of Angles," there is a corresponding mania in our Raceland regarding racial identity. Just as Flatland's inhabitants must be able to infer correctly each other's shapes or risk chaos, in Raceland we are told that everyone must have a "clear racial identity" in order to be healthy psychologically and accepted socially. This notion of a clear racial identity is bound up with psychological and sociological justifications for multiracial ideology. It is also bound up with the need for whites to be able to ascertain who is who racially in order for the door of whiteness to remain guarded.

Biological race is of course the driving principle as this alleged need for a clear racial identity is articulated, for appeals to race as a social construct serve merely to reify the same biological racial categories that were debunked scientifically decades ago. Brown is once again helpful in displaying how the old pathology trope has now been reversed: "With the interracial baby boom that occurred after the demise of antimiscegenation laws in 1967, the social and legal invisibility of biracial children and its consequences became increasingly apparent to those concerned with their well being. Mental health professionals and social scientists began to study interracial children and concluded that the 'one drop of black blood' rule undermines their ability to form clear racial identities."[14]

Beyond the absolutely frightening image conjured up by the prospect of mental health professionals and social scientists let loose on a new and defenseless community, we are left with questions. What precisely is a clear racial identity? Would an explicitly nonracial identity be an acceptably clear one? Why is a biracial identity clear or correct for a person of black/white parentage but a black identity not? On what basis have these mental health professionals and social scientists determined that a multiracial identity is the ideal? Would they be as opposed to a black/white person assuming a white identity as they are to the same person assuming a black identity? As Tanya Hernández suggests, there may be more than just pseudopsychology operating here: "It seems to me that the popular assumption that a child is owed a specific identity reveals as much or more about the needs and privileges of adults than about the needs, rights or ontological reality of human young. In particular, this assumption reflects adults' own socially created needs and contexts that do not deeply threaten their own wishes for communities of like-minded persons who can share and appreciate their identities."[15]

Kerry Ann Rockquemore and David Brunsma have shown that an explicit multiracial identity is but one of at least four possible identity choices made by persons of black/white parentage.[16] Moreover, in further groundbreaking work, Rockquemore and Tracey Laszloffy demonstrate that the full process through which multiracial individuals go in selecting their identities is far more important than whatever identity is selected ultimately.[17] When Patricia Brummet and Loretta Winters explain that the "context with which understanding of race comes to be at any given time or in any given place may be more important to whether multiracial people exhibit mental health or pathology than the actual designation of multiracial itself," they give voice to the reality that we are dealing with an issue far more complicated than the simplistic assertion that persons of mixed parentage need to incorporate both parts of their biological heritage in order to achieve clear racial identities.[18] Writing from a legal context, Twila Perry injects similar complexity into this often far too simplistic debate by noting that "although mental health professionals agree that a positive racial identity is important, there is room for differences of opinion on the question as to what precisely that is."[19]

Nevertheless, Brown asserts that due to hypodescent, "the integration of partial identifications into a unified identity configuration, which according to Erik Erickson (1959) is the hallmark of healthy identity development, was undermined."[20] The key here lies in accepting that blackness and whiteness are real biological essences that have a psychological component, that they are significant partial identifications in the mental health sense implied above, and that in black/white persons they must be unified as Brown describes, in order for such persons to be

healthy mentally. It seems to me that Brown's assertion is overly simplistic and open to scrutiny, however. It seems to me to be a clear
instance of psychobabble.

One might be prompted to ask how dare I write such things. My
answer is that we should resist the urge to accept outlandish propositions merely because psychologists, psychotherapists, or sociologists
have put them forward. It is natural, to be sure, to assume that psychologists know what they are talking about when they are making psychological claims in published texts; however, we should be no more
impressed with Brown's recycling of Erickson than we should be, for
instance, with the ridiculous claim put forth in 1972 by the National
Association of Black Social Workers (and reiterated by that same organization in 1985 congressional testimony) that Afro-American children
being adopted by white parents is tantamount to genocide, and that those
children are better off remaining institutionalized as opposed to being
adopted transracially.[21] Professional and educational statuses by themselves offer no guarantee that people are stating intelligent things that
we should heed as opposed to ridiculous things that we should not.
Ultimately, all claims should be scrutinized, mine included.

In regard to Brown's claims, there has first of all never been any
actual, reliable, nonclinical evidence demonstrating that black/white
persons have truly been tragically conflicted and mentally ill through
the centuries. The tragic mulatto myth has grown as a result of folklore,
as a result of psychological projection by whites who find comfort in the
idea of black/white individuals striving to be white, as a result of
maudlin literature, and as a result of the racist scholarship of academics
such as Edward Reuter. Even Brown herself only cites conclusions
based on clinical studies of "a few interracial families and their children," which of course would be unrepresentative of the broader population of black/white persons, especially considering that the studies in
question were carried out in "mental health clinics" and then unjustifiably generalized "to the overall population of mixed race families." And
of course we may recall from Chapter 1 the nongeneralizability of
Brown's own study as well.

Indeed, if we step back for a moment and consider what is really
being asserted by Brown in her evocation of Erickson—that generations
and generations of black/white persons have quite literally been mentally ill (victims of either of the two pathology tropes) over the centuries—
we begin to gain an appreciation of how preposterous the assertion truly
is. One need not be a licensed psychotherapist to understand this fact, as
it should be patently obvious to anyone possessing an inquiring mind.

Given that this hugely problematic proposition provides the foundation for Brown's work in *The Interracial Experience,* that work must be seen as suspect at the very least.

Let there be no mistake concerning this. In making reference to the Office of Management and Budget's 1997 change from a "mark one only" to a "mark all that apply" approach to federal racial categorization, Brown contends that "for first-generation racially mixed people, the freedom to embrace openly and publicly both parts of their racial heritage promises to be the most important step in smoothing their path toward a clear racial identity and healthy self-esteem."[22] Moreover, she asserts that the "ability for mixed-race people to check all the categories that identify their racial background promises to end their confusion about who they are racially."[23] Here is one of the many places where persons concerned about academic integrity must not allow dubiousness to pass unchallenged, as there is absolutely no reason to believe that checking a box (or multiple boxes) on a form will end any confused person's confusion. It is, after all, a mere form; and someone who truly is confused in the very serious way Brown is suggesting will need far more than a sheet of paper to provide the requisite therapy. This is what Hernández means when she offers that "labels themselves cannot 'other' a group of people."[24] Well taken also is Mary Texeira's unanswerable challenge that supporters of multiracial identity "do not (or cannot?) provide empirical evidence that individual self-esteem is in any way connected to official government racial labels."[25]

Like Brown, G. Reginald Daniel also attempts to link paper and psychotherapy by declaring that "the inclusion of a multiracial identifier, no matter what the format, will not only provide a more accurate picture of contemporary demographics but also help alleviate the psychological oppression imbedded in current methods of data collection, which support and are supported by the one-drop rule."[26] Olumide is again helpful in understanding that there would in the first place be no racial identity problems at all were we not ourselves wedded pathologically to the fantasy of race: "Whatever the social experiences arising from the social construction of mixed race, these are not intrinsic to the population but arise from social processes that create, enable and sustain race thinking and the racialisation of difference."[27] It bears recognizing as well that hyperbolic language such as "psychological oppression" in regard to the marking of a form does little to advance the proidentity argument in a serious way.

My larger point, though, is that Brown endorses the tragic mulatto myth, and suggests quite literally that millions of Afro-Americans have in fact been mentally ill throughout the centuries due to the absence of federal recognition of multiracial identity. Brown's status as a white woman making allusions such as this on behalf of her own mixed-race children is a problematic situation in my view. I acknowledge the touchiness of the subject, but I also am cognizant that the very touchiness of it has resulted in people being unwilling to discuss it as it should be discussed. The time for the awkward silence on this topic to end has long since passed. I will take up the problem of white mothers more generally in Chapter 3, but I want to make note here of the troubling issue raised by a white woman presuming to write about black/white persons because she has children who are mixed-race, and presuming as well to define as mentally ill generations of Afro-Americans both living and dead.

Too many persons, academics as well as nonacademics, are either afraid or unwilling to challenge psychobabble and socioblather when they encounter it. When Brown writes of the "consolidation of black and white identity parts into a unified identity gestalt," we should know that we are face-to-face with psychobabble, and we should be willing to not only identify it as such but to confront and challenge it as well.[28] The entire psychosocio industry of race is founded on a biological fallacy and propounded via academic psychobabble and socioblather. One need not be a psychologist or sociologist to see this; indeed, it may be helpful that one specifically *not* be a practitioner of one of those disciplines in order to appreciate this truth fully.

Socioblather, as I mentioned above, typically begins where psychobabble leaves off. Socioblather takes the presumption that biological race is real (appeals to race as socially determined notwithstanding), that people are identified correctly only when they identify with their proper biological race, and that this racial identity must be validated by society at large in order for the individual to have a meaningful social existence. The individual is seen as too weak to stand against society's will to impose a proper racial identity, resulting in the assumption that our identities must be validated externally in order for us to exist socially.

The notion of validation plays a prominent role in the multiracial identity movement, and it is not surprising that this should be so in the current US culture of entitlement, validation, and perpetual refusal to accept personal responsibility. Everything, it seems, is someone else's responsibility—from the hot coffee we spill in our own laps to the unhealthy fast food we choose to consume to the cigarettes we light and place to our lips. Now, finally, we want the federal government to tell us who we are so that we may feel validated, as we have become too weak to stand up ourselves and state who it is that we are. The sad truth is that in addition to being the Entitlement Generation, we are the Validation Generation.

Kathleen Korgen provides an example of this dependence on others for the validation of our own personal identity when she writes that "according to Cooley's idea of the 'looking glass self,' we are what we think people see [1902]."[29] As I described above, this component of socioblather presumes that a person cannot have an identity that is not recognized and validated by the larger society. In other words, according to Korgen I cannot declare that race is a fallacy and that I therefore have no race, for US society expects that everyone will have a biological racial identity. Therefore, I cannot exist as a functioning member of society until I accept whatever racial identity society will both recognize and validate for me.

Of course, the "looking glass self" is socioblather. While it may certainly hold true for some, it can be quite easily shown, and via several perfectly relevant examples, to be anything but a universal principle. Imagine a racial skeptic, someone who does not believe in biological race. This person is nonetheless very well aware that many of the people looking at him do in fact believe in biological race and see him as a biologically black male. Are we to suppose, then, that our racial skeptic therefore sees himself as they see him—as a biologically black male? To take another example, is it the case that a female Afro-American walking through an upscale boutique actually sees herself as a shoplifter merely because the white salespeople and security staff see her that way? Does their baseless following of her and detaining of her cause her to see herself as a criminal?

Did those graduate and professional students who bravely and by themselves integrated previously segregated institutions of higher learning long before the 1954 Supreme Court decision *Brown v. Board of Education of Topeka* feel that they truly were what their classmates saw them as? Finally, if Korgen's "looking glass self" were something other than socioblather, rather than lending academic support to the idea of multiracial identity, she should be arguing instead that black/white persons are black since they themselves are well aware that this is how the vast majority of Americans see them. Indeed, perhaps the most effective counterexample to Korgen's evocation of the "looking glass self" is the very fact that some black/white persons expend so much emotional capital arguing that they are multiracial and not black.

Perhaps as a universal principle the "looking glass self" made sense to people in 1902, but it seems to me to be opposed radically to the current realities of a truly conscious individuality. It is a justification of, and an apology for, the willful and hegemonic enslavement of some to the opinions of others, and as such serves as one of the underpinnings of our Raceland fantasy. This is truly sad for those unfortunate enough to believe such nonsense. Theories such as this do little more than serve as enablers for the weak-willed to act out their validation needs, as opposed to standing on their own feet and declaring with firmness who they think they are—whether multiracial, monoracial, or nonracial. Korgen's work, as well as the work of others in this vein, also provides both a motivation and an excuse for white mothers of black/white children to complain that without a federal multiracial category their children will not know who they (the children) are.

When Korgen writes approvingly that "[George] McCall and [J. L.] Simmons warn us of the necessity of having a clearly discernible identity in our impersonal society," she adds additional kindling to this fallacious fire.[30] Frankly, the notion of having an identity that is *not* "clearly discernible" is a much more attractive prospect, in my view. It certainly seems superior to agreeing with McCall, Simmons, and Korgen that I require the approbation of society at large in order for my own personal identity to be valid. There is something distinctly distasteful and humiliating in the idea of requesting society's validation and permission in order for me to be who it is I believe I am.

The fact is that society can only approve of and validate our identities if we allow it to, if we relinquish our own power to do so, if we give up an important aspect of our autonomy and moral agency. There will always be people who disagree with our personal identity choices. The question is whether we ought to grant such people the power to alter and determine those personal identity choices for us. If we do, then the term "personal identity" may in fact be a misnomer. I am certainly not denying that there are people, indeed many people, who have surrendered their personal responsibility for determining who they are and have instead allowed society to tell them who they are. But rather than point to these people as examples of society's validating power, I suggest that they—as well as the academics who propound this particular variety of socioblather—be challenged instead of enabled.

Having said that, I want to step back and make two clarifying points. One is related to matters that are more practical and the other to those that are more emotional. The first point is that there is of course a sense in which societal structures do provide frameworks that many people adhere to. Because of this adherence, we are all impacted and affected by those frameworks, even when they are based on fallacious notions of race and racial identity, for instance. When I am in a department store and the clerk at a counter ignores me and chooses instead to serve a customer who quite clearly arrived after I did, I may recognize that I am being affected by a societal structure. I may recognize that the clerk perceives me as black and is likely exhibiting some level of racism. I may recognize as well that I do not have much power in this situation to alter either the clerk's belief in race or the clerk's inclination to a racist response toward me. I could certainly lecture the clerk on the falsity of the racial enterprise, but it would surely represent a quixotic venture on my part.

Yet even though I recognize my placement in this odious and misguided societal structure of race and racism, such recognition does not imply that I must myself acquiesce in that structure. I do not have to accept the black racial identity the racist clerk has assigned to me any more than I have to accept the clerk's racism. In this case my response to the former is internal while the response to the latter will most likely be external. In terms of the former I will continue secure in my knowledge that race is a fallacy despite the actions of this silly clerk toward me. In terms of the latter I will reject the clerk's racism in a more outward way, as my usual response to a situation of this type is to inquire rather loudly as to whether there is some reason a person has chosen to ignore me in order to help someone who obviously arrived after I did.

Clearly, there are situations that are far less trivial than the one I have provided here, situations that may even rise to the level of life or death. I do not mean to trivialize those more serious situations, which for reasons of personal safety may even necessitate giving the impression of at least temporarily acquiescing in the societal structure. My point is that while I do recognize that I can be impacted negatively by certain social structures, this recognition is no reason for me to accept internally, nor is it in most cases any reason to accept externally, that society has the power to dictate my identity to me. To put it another way, being *in* the societal structure does not necessarily require being *of* it.

The second clarifying point is that I do in fact understand and appreciate the true anguish some people feel because they believe in biological race and because they are not strong enough to be who they are without some form of validation from others. When Brown writes that "trying to fit into the socially prescribed mold that can only accommodate half of who the interracial child is seems to be an enormous struggle," there is actually a sense in which she is correct.[31] It can indeed be a struggle if we allow ourselves to become caught up in belief in biological race and in kowtowing to the wishes of other people to prescribe racial identities for us. If one truly believes that the biological union of this particular egg and that particular sperm actually results in a child that is really half white and half black, and that in order to be healthy mentally this child must live a life that somehow incorporates and maintains a proper balance of those two biological halves in a "unified identity gestalt," then a lifetime of adjustment problems may indeed be in store. We might be inclined to agree with Olumide and "hazard a hypothesis here, that what are commonly termed 'identity problems' among those considered to be mixed or mixing are a temporary victory of social sanctions over individual attempts at self-identification."[32]

Life can certainly be hard, especially for children, but we do our children no favors by teaching them that they are what other people say they are, or that they must have a racial identity (whether multiracial or monoracial) because society will not accept them without one. This goes for Afro-American pressure to identify as black as well as for parental pressure to identify as multiracial. Afro-Americans may demand that a person of black/white parentage identify as black against her or his wishes, and such demands ought to be rejected. Similarly, peer pressure for a person of black/white parentage to identify as multiracial ought to be rejected as well. Unfortunately, parental indoctrination to identify as multiracial is a much more powerful force and cannot be rejected until much later, if at all. It is enough to say here that parental indoctrination is another attempt to impose identity; yet, as is the case with the role of white mothers generally, it has apparently been too touchy an issue to discuss. I shall address it in Chapter 3, however.

Renee Romano relates an interesting example of our Validation Generation in writing about an interracial couple and a now-defunct mixed-race-oriented magazine: "This kind of reinforcement and support can fill a need couples were not even aware of. As one interracial couple wrote from Atlanta, before they discovered *Interrace,* 'Neither of us had realized how much we need the kind of validity that *Interrace* provides.'"[33] The fortuitous discovery of validation that one did not realize one needed is truly a fascinating thing to consider. It is one thing to discover a resource that one was unaware of previously, and to make use of and appreciate that resource. It is quite something else, however, to be willing to state that one did not realize one needed validation until coming across a particular magazine. Yet this is what our culture of validation has brought us to. I also think it a fair assumption that this couple will pass on to any children they might have their view as to the importance of external validation of personal identity.

There are a number of faulty beliefs bound up together that work to produce arguments for multiracial identity. These beliefs revolve around acceptance of biological race, the need for external validation of personal identity, the quest for a federal multiracial category, and a concerted refusal to consider alternative identity options. Within this mix, there is a distinct privileging of multiracial identity, as well as a distinct unprivileging of monoracial identity—particularly black identity. Rockquemore reports that there are at least four distinct identities chosen by black/white persons: a singular identity (exclusively black), a border identity (exclusively biracial), a protean identity (multiple identities), and a transcendent identity (beyond race).[34] As Rockquemore relates, these are the different ways black/white persons identify themselves, and "those who do not choose a border identity are still multiracial by ancestry. However, their choices of racial identification are not only ignored by multiracial advocates, but the community's silence on the legitimate existence of alternative racial self-understandings has the effect of simultaneously privileging the border identity, and delegitimizing all other identity options."[35]

Marion Kilson demonstrates this inherent bias when she consistently describes as a negative identity a person's choice to not adopt any racial identity at all: "In roughly equal numbers, individuals have changed from a negative racial identity (such as 'Other' or 'Unknown') to either a positive affirmation of an identity of color or to a positive affirmation of all of their racial heritages."[36] Yet why should the decision to opt for a raceless identity be described in negative terms, and why should the decision to adopt a societally validated (or imposed) racial identity be classed platitudinously as a "positive affirmation"? The love affair certain academics have with the concept of race, and their utter inability to release themselves from its grasp, are displayed in characterizations such as this.

Even though Kilson at one point acknowledges that some multiracial persons "may assume a raceless identity from a conscious lack of interest in claiming a racial identity," she nonetheless continues to categorize such a choice negatively.[37] Her normative bias toward acceptance of biological race as real is evident in her glowing descriptions of what she considers to be a proper identity choice: "Although some of the Biracial young adults in the study continue to struggle to achieve self-acceptance, most have developed a self-affirming racial identity."[38] What sounds like careful, academic prose here is no more than wishful thinking, though, as a "self-affirming racial identity" has no basis in reality, and is instead psychobabble deployed in support of both biological race and multiracial identity.

The effect of our affirmation/validation culture is apparent here, and is reflected as well in the words of Deborah Ramirez, who offers that "multiracial people view identity as multidimensional and deserve acknowledgment and appreciation of all their heritages."[39] One often heard this sort of sentiment from nonscholar activists in the earlier days of the movement, and it is somewhat surprising to find an academic displaying in so overt a way the same mawkish attitudes.[40] The notion that people "deserve acknowledgment" of their heritages is a fairly common sentiment, but this hardly makes it sensible as opposed to merely bathetic. How can people possibly be said to deserve "appreciation of all of their heritages"? Shall I be forced to appreciate all of your heritages? Shall you be forced to appreciate all of mine? How am I to know if your stated appreciation is sincere, or would this even matter as long as your appreciation is expressed?

Appealing as well to the notion of racial heritages, Brown writes of racial status laws "pushing participants toward blackness and disregarding the other half of their racial makeup," but this assertion needs to be unpacked and assessed.[41] Brown is correct that the US racial paradigm does prescribe identities for persons of black/white parentage using the formula of hypodescent, whereby the mixed-race child takes on the racial identity of the parent of lower racial status. However, rather than assenting to the madness of biological race, we could instead take the progressive step of refusing to accept hypodescent, the paradigm, and its assigned identities. Anthropologists and geneticists have long since moved beyond the 1950s on the subject of biological race; imagine if sociologists and psychologists joined them! Of course, such progressivism would put many of the latter two groups out of work, but given the theories some of those particular academics are propounding we would all surely be the better for that particular outcome.

When Korgen informs us that "noted psychologists and psychiatrists have come 'to the opinion that for a person of mixed ancestry to neglect one or the other parent's identity [is] to detract from a clear racial identity,'" my admittedly inelegant response is to reply in return that noted psychologists and psychiatrists are perfectly capable of propagating nonsense.[42] When Daniel tells us that "according to Los Angeles psychologist Patricia Johnson, the psychic development of multiracial-identified individuals is different from that of single-race identified individuals," we might be inclined at first to be somewhat impressed.[43] However, when we learn from Daniel's relevant endnote that he gleaned this information from the *Oprah Winfrey Show* of October 7, 1994, it casts this particular psychological newsflash in a somewhat different light.[44]

It is our responsibility as thinking human beings and as academics to review the evidence and decide for ourselves what makes sense and what does not. To shirk this responsibility is to risk being fed absurdities, for which all fault lies with oneself. We are each the ultimate arbiters of what we choose to believe, and we should take that responsibility seriously. Toward that end I ask, which, after all, is the more outlandish proposition—standing up and asserting that neither biological race nor multirace are real and that we ought not to give them credence, or asserting that persons of black/white parentage must consolidate the biopsychic essences of their two racial halves into a "unified identity gestalt"? For me, the choice is more than clear.

Among academics writing in support of multiracial identity there has developed a distinct culture of victimization or debilitation in regard to children of black/white parentage. It essentially is another facet of the neopathology trope. As with many other aspects of the proidentity position, this culture of special weakness is articulated by proidentity academics without the slightest evidence and is never challenged. It is simply taken for granted without argument. This culture holds that black/white children have "special needs" that seem to divide into those related specifically to race mixture and those related to racial discrimination, although the two often merge. I find it particularly fascinating that this special needs argument resurrects the old, nineteenth-century falsity that mulattoes were weaker than either blacks or whites, demonstrating even further that the pathology trope has not really been changed at all.

Writing near the middle of the twentieth century, Gunnar Myrdal cataloged what were seen as the special needs of mulattoes at that time, including the assertions that they "tend to be sterile; that they—having parents of two distinct races—are not harmoniously proportioned, but have a trait of one parent side by side with a trait of the other parent, paired in such a way that the two cannot function together properly; that they are more susceptible to tuberculosis; that, because Negroes have relatively long, narrow heads, Negro women, with narrow pelvises, and their mulatto offspring are endangered when they bear children of white men whose heads are rounder, and so on."[45] So the mantra of special needs is something of an echo from an earlier time—less outrageous, less related to the physical, but no less false.

Brown cites the special needs of her own children as a motivation for conducting her study. According to Brown, her "children were good teachers, but [she] would have welcomed some external support system or professional or literary guidance that focused on the experiences and the special needs of mixed-race children. Since these were virtually non-existent, creating an environment that would foster a healthy identity frequently became a matter or trial and error."[46] That certainly seems a frightening way to raise children of any background; however, I would very seriously suggest that the nonexistence of specific instruction manuals for black/white children is no more of a problem than the lack of specific manuals for white or for black children. Just as the claim that black/white persons are healthier psychologically if they identify as multiracial is asserted without credible evidence, the claim that black/white children have special needs is likewise never argued for. It is simply stated, as Romano does when writing about multiracial family organizations as being "particularly interested in nurturing biracial children and helping families meet their children's unique developmental needs."[47]

Paul Rosenblatt, Terri Karis, and Richard Powell offer an astonishing example of the resounding emptiness of the special needs claim in a study they conducted on black and white multiracial families. Notice how the authors literally insist that black/white children have special needs, despite no evidence to support the claim: "As far as could be determined from what parents said, the children were living normal, healthy lives. Nonetheless, racism can pose challenges for an interracial couple raising a child."[48] And again, sounding almost disappointed to find the black/white children in their study to be without major problems, the authors relate that "by all accounts, the children of these couples were consistently doing well. Nonetheless, parenting biracial children can pose challenges."[49] On the question of racism posing challenges for raising multiracial children, Hernández delivers an incisive point, reminding us that the "anguish experienced by targets of racial bias is not a dynamic peculiar to the 'culture' of mixed race persons."[50] Along these same lines, Texeira is critical of the discourse of the "multiracial agenda," referring to it as "a kind of 'racism light,' a scholarship that takes little note of structural power (other than the government census), but that offers as the most profound effects of racism the lack of 'a place for them.'"[51]

Unless we are considering racial bias coming from other nonwhites, if a black/white child is the subject of racial discrimination it very likely can only be because of that child's nonwhite ancestry. In this sense, that discrimination is no different than the racial discrimination directed at Afro-Americans every day. Linking ordinary racial discrimination to some assumed special needs of black/white children is not legitimate, in my view. Nonetheless, Brown links the two in order to create a special need where there is none, or at least none any more special than that for any Afro-American child: "In some other schools, however, teachers were not only ignorant about the special needs of interracial children, but they failed to confront racist abuses."[52] These are two different questions that have nothing to do with each other.

The first question (the undocumented case for special needs) is a fallacy about which nothing can or should be done, while the second question (confronting racism) should be dealt with no differently than for any victim of racism. One might be led, though, to imagine that racists really do care about calculating the amounts of varying ancestry in their victims' personal histories when Brown advises that due to "their ambiguous racial status and their vulnerability to discrimination, the interracial child has some special needs."[53] If the black/white child is the victim of racism coming from whites, we can be reasonably sure that the racism is directed at the victim's nonwhite ancestry, and not the victim's white ancestry. As Hernández reminds us, "the racial hierarchy tends to view biracial persons as inferior, not because they are mixed-race, but because they are non-white."[54]

Joining the special needs chorus, Maria Root asks how parents are to "equip their children, then, to defend themselves against the childhood taunts of oreos, coconuts, apples, zebras, and half-breeds? While a parent of color may have been subjected to name calling, what sets her or his children apart is that they may be called names by people from their own racial groups."[55] Frankly, I find Root's concern here particularly uncompelling. Taunts are taunts no matter what their source, and I would venture that it is no more or less hurtful for a person of one's own perceived racial group to deliver a racial taunt than it is for a person of one's own perceived racial group to deliver any other kind of taunt. In fact, while psychologists studying race and multirace tend to overemphasize the pain of racial taunts, it may well be that a racial taunt delivered by a person of one's own perceived racial group is far less hurtful to a particular child at a particular point in time than being called fat, ugly, stupid, or any other number of insults by that same person.

Root adds that "parenting is challenging no matter what, particularly for parents of mixed-heritage children. These parents are told that they must discuss race in order to prepare their children to meet the world."[56] Of course, if psychologists such as Root and Brown did not assure parents of this very dubious "necessity," the concern would become quickly moot. I instead find myself in agreement with Texeira's progressive suggestion that the anxieties of a black/white child "might be better addressed by the child's parents who must convey to the child that race and skin color are individual genetic variables, not group markers in need of official government imprimatur."[57] Certainly I do not deny that at some points in their lives black/white children may not want to be seen with their white mothers (to invoke that example), for instance. I ask, however, how very much different is this kind of phase from other such events in childhood development? Children may not want to be seen with a parent who is overweight, who is unattractive, who dresses poorly, or who has a strong body odor. Indeed, a child may not want to be seen with a parent for no other reason than simply because that person is in fact her or his parent.

None of this is to make light of the situation of a black/white child not wanting to be seen with her or his white mother at some particular developmental phase. Rather, it is to bring into perspective this particular issue and to ask if effective resolution really requires the efforts of psychologists, psychotherapists, and specific multiracial indoctrination at the levels Brown, Daniel, Kilson, Korgen, and Root suggest. I do not believe it does. Not every phase of life requires psychological intervention, no more than every personal condition requires medication, as we can overpsychologize every bit as much as we can overmedicate, all to our own detriment. Some issues simply take care of themselves in the normal course of things. As Texeira points out, "there is little evidence to suggest that biracial children suffer any more than children whose parents are of one heritage."[58]

I again raise the concern regarding past generations of black/white persons. How reasonable is it to imply that suddenly all of this psychosocio intervention is now required in the lives of black/white individuals? One wonders how we ever made it to adulthood as contributing members of society in the days before white female academics such as Brown, Kilson, and Korgen came on the scene to decree how we should be raised—with every colonial impulse and every psychological projection implied. When Root declares that "in reality, many parents cannot provide the map the child needs for negotiating the world as a child of mixed heritage," I answer that love, intelligence, and common sense are far superior to any maps psychologists might come up with.[59]

Nor is there a case to be made for white parents not being skillful enough to deal with racism, as Brown suggests here: "Never having gone through life as a person of color, the white parent may not react to racism the way a black person does. Consequently, he or she may lack the necessary coping skills and may feel anxious or inadequate in teaching a child how to survive in a racist environment."[60] The "coping skills" myth, which was long ago debunked by Ann Wilson (1987) and by Barbara Tizard and Ann Phoenix (1993), is an extraordinary insult to white parents, and demonstrates the excruciatingly low level of academic discourse we are dealing with here, and which this book is seeking to provide a corrective for.[61] Are we to imagine honestly, is it being suggested seriously, that *any* Afro-American parent is necessarily more skilled at dealing with racism directed at her or his black/white child than *any* white parent would be?

The coping skills myth has a long history in the controversies surrounding racial identity and the transracial adoption of Afro-American children by white parents, predating the modern multiracial identity debate by decades. It is old and discredited news, and the fact that Brown invokes it contemporarily with no apparent appreciation of its fictive status is a concern. One of the typical lines of argument against transracial adoption was the idea of white parents being incapable of teaching certain "survival strategies" to Afro-American children, as explained by Peter Hayes in an article challenging that notion: "The claim that TRA [transracial adoption] is a threat to mental health is supported by a theory that minority communities, and in particular the African American community, have responded to endemic societal racism by developing 'survival strategies' that involve practicing an amoral 'seduction' of dominant society."[62]

As an example, Leon Chestang presents just this type of argument when he asks, "Can white parents equip a black child for the inevitable assaults on his personality from a society that considers his color to be enough reason to reject him? Can they learn to do this without having internalized the duality of character so necessary for survival? How can the black child learn the necessary maneuvering, seduction, self-enhancement through re-definition, and many other tactics taught by black parents, by word and deed, directly and indirectly?"[63] But the fact is that, Chestang's rantings aside, there are no such particular strategies that are the exclusive province of Afro-American parents. The notion that there is some sort of scripted formula to be handed down, or that all Afro-American parents even manage to cope successfully themselves with racism to the same degree, is simply insupportable.

Not all Afro-American parents have been victims of direct racism, and even for those who have been, there is no reason at all to suppose that, by itself, this experience makes them better capable, compared to any particular white parent, of converting those experiences into useful lessons for their children. The coping skills myth truly is racial stereotyping of the highest (or would it be the lowest?) order, as we should just as easily be able to imagine Afro-American parents who have been victims of direct racism but who would be not good at all at preparing their children to deal with racial discrimination, as well as white parents who have never been victims of racism but who would be quite good at such preparation. I sincerely hope that the goal would not be for a white parent to "react to racism the way a black person does" (do they all react the same way?), but rather to react to racism intelligently and with love for one's children in mind, regardless of racial classification. After all, some Afro-Americans react to racism in a variety of unfortunate ways that we surely would not want their children to emulate. Yet when we are mired at this level of discourse, we have to fight to see even so clearly evident a point.

In a racially mixed sample of mothers of black/white children, about 72 percent of whom were white, Wilson found that "the more forcefully she represented systematic racial bias to her child, the less likely her child was to experience a racial identity conflict." [64] Tizard and Phoenix, also in a racially mixed sample of mothers of black/white children, about 80 percent of whom were white, found even more powerful results in refuting the coping skills myth: "We found no evidence that, according to their children, black and white parents gave different advice, used different strategies themselves, or communicated more or less about racism. Black parents were no more likely than white parents to tell the young people they should be proud of their colour."[65] "From the young people's accounts it was clear that the ways in which they dealt with racism, their 'survival strategies,' were no different from the ways in which we all deal with situations perceived as potentially threatening or painful."[66] "The young people seemed to have no one set of 'survival skills' for dealing with racism. They used the range of coping mechanisms which all of us use to deal with potentially threatening situations, most frequently ignoring racist abuse or returning it. . . . We did not find that the young people growing up with a black parent used different strategies from the others. We did not find, either, that black parents were transmitting different ways of dealing with racism from those suggested by white parents."[67]

What becomes painfully clear is that something other than merely being the parent or relative of a black/white child is required if one is going to engage in academically sound scholarly discourse on the topic of multiracial identity. Having multiracial children or relatives does not by itself impart knowledge of the research already published in this particular field of study. It certainly does not eliminate the necessity of being aware of the current state of the literature. Beyond the necessity of being cognizant of the different ideological positions various writers may take on the issues, there is also a need to be knowledgeable about things that are simply objective fact. Being connected to the literature ensures that one is up-to-date in regard to both of these aspects, as when one is not connected, disinformation is the likely result.

For example, in a chapter titled "Public Policy Implications," Korgen lists three "issues" or "uncertainties" that she describes as having "stoked the fire of the current debate over a potential multiracial category in the Census 2000": discrimination, affirmative action, and the 2000 census itself.[68] But the promise of the chapter's title is an empty one, as the ensuing discussion has nothing at all to do with any issues that generated controversy over a federal multiracial category and the Census 2000 from a public policy standpoint.

During the sometimes contentious debates leading up to the 2000 census, discrimination against multiracial persons was occasionally brought up by multiracial advocacy organizations, but in response it was always quickly and effectively pointed out that discrimination against multiracial people is always discrimination directed against that element of the victim's ancestry that the racist hates, and not discrimination against multiracial identity independent of that particular ancestry. So in the general debate, discrimination against multiracials was not an issue, nor does Korgen's discussion offer anything substantially different from the preceding. Affirmative action represented even less of an issue in the census debate. And it is difficult to make sense of Korgen's assertion that the 2000 census was one of the "issues" or "uncertainties" that "stoked the fire of the current debate over a potential multiracial category in the Census 2000," as it seems to be something of a circular statement.

The single most important issue of the debate over a federal multiracial category and the 2000 census, from a public policy perspective, was civil rights compliance monitoring, which is not the same thing as the very narrow topic of supposed discrimination against multiracial people. Among many other things, this issue concerned the origins of the federal racial categories in tracking those groups who have suffered historical oppression at the hands of the US government, the future usefulness of the massive racial statistics collected over the past several decades, the ability to transfer consistent and comparable racial statistical data between federal agencies, and questions of how to ensure the continued ability to track discrimination and to monitor compliance with existing civil rights laws should federal racial categories be altered in any way. For Korgen to purport to discuss the "public policy implications" of a federal multiracial category vis-à-vis the 2000 census, but to make no mention of civil rights compliance monitoring, is simply unfathomable.[69] Yet this is the result of not being connected to the current literature of the field. Whether one is writing about objective facts as in the preceding example, or about ideological issues, knowing what is already out there is critical.

One need not agree necessarily with the work that has already been done; indeed, one could not possibly agree with all of it in so polarized a field. However, academics seeking to publish work on multiracial identity have a professional obligation to those who have gone before, and to their own research subjects as well, to have enough respect for the field itself to at least become familiar with this area of study prior to writing about it. This is no less than what one would expect in the disciplines of anthropology, history, or philosophy. It is time that the field of multiracial identity studies demanded the same level of academic competence from its participants—particularly those writing from sociological or psychological backgrounds—as do these other fields of scholarly inquiry.

Such a demand for the highest levels of scholarly competence would result in the interrogation and problematization of certain dubious assertions and assumptions that ordinarily inspire not even the least bit of pause on the proidentity front, and that facilitate the perpetuation of the Raceland fantasy in which we find ourselves. In Chapter 3, I shall highlight several such assertions and assumptions specifically concerning the touchy issue of white mothers of black/white children, and of the impact of those mothers on the racial identity formation of their children. This will allow us to discern a link between the emotion-laden interests of activist white mothers on the one hand and current proidentity scholarship on the other, a link that will play an important role in one of my major arguments of Chapter 4.

Notes

1. Edwin Abbott, *Flatland: A Romance of Many Dimensions,* 2nd ed. (London: Seeley, 1884; reprint, New York: Penguin, 1998), 36.
2. Ibid., 36, 37.
3. The work of these three scholars is invoked often in arguments supporting multiracial identity.
4. Edward Reuter, *The Mulatto in the United States: Including a Study of the Rôle of Mixed-Blood Races Throughout the World* (Boston: Richard G. Badger, 1918; reprint, New York: Negro Universities Press, 1969); Fannie Hurst, *Imitation of Life* (New York: Harper, 1933).
5. For several examples of such multiracial identity models, see Rainier

Spencer, "Beyond Pathology and Cheerleading: Insurgency, Dissolution, and Complicity in the Multiracial Idea," in *The Politics of Multiracialism: Challenging Racial Thinking*, ed. Heather M. Dalmage (Albany: State University of New York Press, 2004), 105–106.

6. Jill Olumide, *Raiding the Gene Pool: The Social Construction of Mixed Race* (London: Pluto, 2002), 51.

7. Ibid., 157.

8. I have elsewhere written more extensively on this particular point: Rainier Spencer, *Spurious Issues: Race and Multiracial Identity Politics in the United States* (Boulder: Westview, 1999), 37–48; Spencer, "Beyond Pathology and Cheerleading," 109.

9. Ursula Brown, *The Interracial Experience: Growing Up Black/White Racially Mixed in the United States* (Westport: Praeger, 2001), 109.

10. It is doubly illegitimate because first, the results of studying a "few interracial families" were generalized to the broader population of multiracial Americans; and second, those few samples were acquired in "mental health clinics."

11. Brown, *The Interracial Experience*, 109.

12. Ibid., 109, 111.

13. Ibid., 43.

14. Ibid., 58–59.

15. Tanya K. Hernández, "'Multiracial' Discourse: Racial Classifications in an Era of Color-Blind Jurisprudence," *Maryland Law Review* 57, no. 97 (1998): 106.

16. Kerry Ann Rockquemore and David Brunsma, *Beyond Black: Biracial Identity in America* (Thousand Oaks, CA: Sage, 2002).

17. Kerry Ann Rockquemore and Tracey Laszloffy, *Raising Biracial Children: From Theory to Practice* (Walnut Creek, CA: Alta Mira, 2005), chap. 1.

18. Patricia O'Donnell Brummett and Loretta Winters, "Gang Affiliation and Self-Esteem: The Effects of a Mixed-Heritage Identity," in *New Faces in a Changing America: Multiracial Identity in the 21st Century*, eds. Loretta Winters and Herman DeBose (Thousand Oaks, CA: Sage, 2003), 338.

19. Twila Perry, "Race and Child Placement: The Best Interests Test and the Cost of Discretion," in *Mixed Race America and the Law: A Reader*, ed. Kevin Johnson (New York: New York University Press, 2003), 347.

20. Brown, *The Interracial Experience*, 1.

21. Rita J. Simon and Howard Altstein, *Adoption, Race, & Identity: From Infancy to Young Adulthood* (New Brunswick, NJ: Transaction, 2002), 14–15, 36 n. 49.

22. Brown, *The Interracial Experience*, 3.

23. Ibid., 52–53.

24. Hernández, "'Multiracial' Discourse," 160.

25. Mary Thierry Texeira, "The New Multiracialism: An Affirmation of or an End to Race As We Know It?" in *New Faces in a Changing America*, eds. Winters and DeBose, 28.

26. G. Reginald Daniel, *More Than Black? Multiracial Identity and the New Racial Order* (Philadelphia: Temple University Press, 2002), 190.

27. Olumide, *Raiding the Gene Pool,* 179–180.

28. Brown, *The Interracial Experience,* 10.

29. Kathleen Korgen, *From Black to Biracial: Transforming Racial Identity Among Americans* (Westport: Praeger, 1999), 5.

30. Ibid., 92.

31. Brown, *The Interracial Experience,* 2–3.

32. Olumide, *Raiding the Gene Pool,* 173.

33. Renee C. Romano, *Race Mixing: Black-White Marriage in Postwar America* (Cambridge: Harvard University Press, 2003), 274.

34. Kerry Ann Rockquemore, "Deconstructing Tiger Woods: The Promise and the Pitfalls of Multiracial Identity," in *The Politics of Multiracialism,* ed. Dalmage, 125–141.

35. Ibid., 134.

36. Marion Kilson, *Claiming Place: Biracial Young Adults of the Post–Civil Rights Era* (Westport: Bergin and Garvey, 2001), 44–45.

37. Ibid., 46.

38. Ibid., 47.

39. Deborah Ramirez, "Multicultural Empowerment: It's Not Just Black and White Anymore," in *Mixed Race America and the Law,* ed. Johnson, 197.

40. Ramirez' article was published originally in 1995, so she was actually writing during the time that many nonscholar activists were expressing the same type of emotionalistic arguments.

41. Brown, *The Interracial Experience,* 59.

42. Korgen, *From Black to Biracial,* 22.

43. Daniel, *More Than Black?* 106.

44. Ibid., 214 n. 58.

45. Gunnar Myrdal, *An American Dilemma: The Negro Problem and Modern Democracy* (New York: Harper and Brothers, 1944), 107.

46. Brown, *The Interracial Experience,* 21.

47. Romano, *Race Mixing,* 280–281.

48. Paul C. Rosenblatt, Terri A. Karis, and Richard Powell, *Multiracial Couples: Black & White Voices* (Thousand Oaks, CA: Sage, 1995), 193.

49. Ibid., 213–214.

50. Hernández, "'Multiracial' Discourse," 114.

51. Texeira, "The New Multiracialism," 33.

52. Brown, *The Interracial Experience,* 87.

53. Ibid., 111.

54. Hernández, "'Multiracial' Discourse," 163.

55. Maria P. P. Root, *Love's Revolution: Interracial Marriage* (Philadelphia: Temple University Press, 2001), 148.

56. Ibid.

57. Texeira, "The New Multiracialism," 33.

58. Ibid., 33.

59. Root, *Love's Revolution,* 152.

60. Brown, *The Interracial Experience,* 112.

61. Anne Wilson, *Mixed Race Children: A Study of Identity* (Boston: Allen and Unwin, 1987); Barbara Tizard and Ann Phoenix, *Black, White, or Mixed Race? Race and Racism in the Lives of Young People of Mixed Parentage*

(London: Routledge, 1993). Both of these studies were conducted in Britain, but there is no reason for supposing that, in the relevant basics, the US situation is any different.

62. Peter Hayes, "Transracial Adoption: Politics and Ideology," *Child Welfare* 72, no. 3 (May–June 1993): 306.

63. Leon Chestang, "The Dilemma of Biracial Adoption," *Social Work* 17, no. 3 (May 1972): 103.

64. Wilson, *Mixed Race Children,* 167.

65. Tizard and Phoenix, *Black, White, or Mixed Race?* 130.

66. Ibid., 108.

67. Ibid., 174–175. Again, while acknowledging that Wilson's study and Tizard and Phoenix's study were conducted in Britain, I would challenge anyone to demonstrate that coping skills are a myth there but are nonetheless a reality in the United States.

68. Korgen, *From Black to Biracial,* 97.

69. National Research Council, Committee on National Statistics, Panel on Census Requirements in the Year 2000 and Beyond, *Modernizing the U.S. Census,* edited by Barry Edmonston and Charles Schultze (Washington, DC: National Academy Press, 1995); US House Subcommittee on Census, Statistics, and Postal Personnel, Committee on Post Office and Civil Service, *Hearings on the Review of Federal Measurements of Race and Ethnicity,* 103rd Cong., 1st sess., April 14, June 30, July 29, November 3, 1993; US House Subcommittee on Government Management, Information, and Technology, Committee on Government Reform and Oversight, *Hearings on Federal Measures of Race and Ethnicity and the Implications for the 2000 Census,* 105th Cong., 1st sess., April 23, May 22, July 25, 1997.

3

White Mothers, the *Loving* Legend, and Manufacturing a Biracial Baby Boom

Before their eyes he changed. He was Tom and James and a man named Switchman, another named Butterfield; and he was the town mayor and the young girl Judith and the husband William and the wife Clarisse. He was melting wax shaping to their minds. They shouted, they pressed forward, pleading. He screamed, threw out his hands, his face dissolving to each demand. "Tom!" cried LaFarge. "Alice!" another. "William!" They snatched his wrists, whirled him about, until with one last shriek of horror he fell. He lay on the stones, melted wax cooling, his face all faces, one eye blue, the other golden, hair that was brown, red, yellow, black, one eyebrow thick, one thin, one hand large, one small. They stood over him and put their fingers to their mouths. They bent down. "He's dead," someone said at last. It began to rain.

—Ray Bradbury, *The Martian Chronicles*[1]

In recent scholarly publications on the topic of multiracial identity, we read over and over about a supposed post-1967 interracial marriage and biracial baby boom resulting directly from the historic Supreme Court decision *Loving v. Commonwealth of Virginia,* and about a newly found freedom to identify "correctly" as multiracial that so many young multiracial adults are nowadays experiencing and taking advantage of. Several authors in recent years—some of whom I have mentioned in earlier chapters, such as Ursula Brown, G. Reginald Daniel, Kathleen Korgen, and Maria Root—have invoked that Supreme Court decision as central to their arguments for multiracial identity. These authors posit a distinction between multiracial people prior to the mid-1960s and multiracial people after the mid-1960s—a distinction tied explicitly to the 1967 *Loving* decision, which invalidated state laws against interracial marriage in the United States.

While it may be possible to make such a pre- and post-*Loving* distinction, and while the distinction may indeed even be useful, it is certainly *not* useful for the reasons cited specifically by the writers who invoke it. Moreover, I am not at all certain that the *Loving* decision should be granted such paradigm-shifting, ideology-changing status in the first place, given that only a few states had current antimiscegenation laws at the time anyway. In other words, while the *Loving* decision was certainly an indisputably important legal event—and I do not intend to undermine its general significance—the alleged pre- and post-*Loving* distinction as regards multiracial identity may nevertheless be yet another of those many unchallenged and unproblematized assumptions that, as we have seen, are so very prevalent in the world of pro–multiracial identity academic writing.

One very serious problem with the position of these writers is that this supposed post-*Loving* multiracial ideology is not backed up by anything approaching hard evidence. In every case I am aware of, the assertion is based on no evidence, on anecdotal evidence, on microscopic and unrepresentative research samples gathered using the snowball technique, or simply on emotional sentiment and wishful thinking. In general, the claim is offered and advanced as if it were thoroughly unproblematic, and then entire books are subsequently built upon this very questionable foundation. The all-too-real danger here is that there are still so few scholarly monographs available on multiracial identity that such error-filled volumes are often allowed, by default, to carry more weight than they otherwise would.

We may begin by verifying that proidentity writers have in fact taken up the *Loving* claim. According to Brown, the *Loving* decision along with the civil rights movement "opened the door to interracial marriages."[2] Daniel attributes growth in interracial marriages to "the *Loving* decision and the comparatively more fluid social relations that followed it."[3] He also makes reference to *Loving* as "a historical marker in the formation of multiracial consciousness."[4] Finally, Korgen cites the *Loving* decision as being the "first and foremost legal influence" leading to an "increase in cross-racial couplings."[5] The presumption is that this increase in interracial marriages is associated with a paradigmatic change in racial attitudes attributable directly to *Loving,* which is then linked to an increase in couples' willingness to identify their children as multiracial, and which is tied subsequently to specific conclusions about the nature of that identity.

Yet as I have noted, no evidence is offered to establish these alleged connections. All that is ever furnished are census data showing the numbers of interracially married couples; however, no causal link is provided to show either that there is in fact a cause-and-effect relationship between the *Loving* decision and a subsequent increase in interracial marriages, or that any increase in interracial marriages since 1967 (particularly black/white marriages) is not the continuation of an ongoing trend already established prior to 1967. Finally, few of the writers touting the *Loving* decision's significance for multiracial identity today have analyzed interracial marriage trends by group to see if particular subpopulations are behaving differently than others in regard to interracial marriage. In fact, according to one scholar who has performed such an analysis, "interracial marriage patterns have changed since *Loving,* but the shifts have differed for blacks, Asian Americans, Native Americans, and Latinos."[6] For instance, in addition to a slight increase in black/white intermarriage rates prior to Loving, "Asian American outmarriage to whites increased steadily well before the Supreme Court declared antimiscegenation laws unconstitutional in *Loving,*" and "rates of marriage between Native Americans and whites were relatively high even before the *Loving* decision."[7]

It also seems reasonable to assume that the *Loving* decision would have had little effect in states where it was already irrelevant due to the absence of antimiscegenation legislation, and should correspondingly have had its greatest impact in those states where existing antimiscegenation laws were invalidated by the decision. In other words, it is not sensible to suppose that significant numbers of interracial couples residing in states where it was legal for them to marry prior to 1967 would have nonetheless refrained from marrying because such marriages were outlawed in other states. *Loving* would not have had much in the way of a direct impact on their decisions to marry, as they were generally already getting married anyway.

Since most of the sixteen states whose antimiscegenation statutes were declared unconstitutional by *Loving* were in the South, it would stand to reason that if *Loving* were responsible for intermarriage increases in the directly causal way presumed by proidentity academics, dramatic increases in interracial marriage after *Loving* would have taken place in Alabama, Mississippi, and the other Deep South states. It is interesting to note then, as Renee Romano does, that in the late twentieth century in Mississippi, South Carolina, and Alabama, "more than 40 percent of the voters cast ballots to retain their state's symbolic constitutional bans on interracial marriage."[8] When this many citizens vote to retain an already unconstitutional law for purely symbolic purposes, one is hard-pressed to find the watershed change in racial attitudes asserted by proidentity academics.

Today, in fact, "only one-third of whites in the South say they approve" of racial intermarriage.[9] This is a significant point, for the couples under consideration did not and are not generally getting married in the South, certainly not in the explosive numbers required for the *Loving* legend to be true. Indeed, in the South, it appears that the "white man's rank order of discriminations" cataloged by Gunnar Myrdal in 1944 remains essentially the same.[10] Certainly the item at the very top of the list, the "bar against intermarriage and sexual intercourse involving white women," has not changed much at all.[11] Even moving outside the South, the situation does not alter dramatically, as "nationwide, approval for black-white intermarriage lags significantly behind that for other forms of integration, such as living in mixed-race neighborhoods or sending one's children to integrated schools."[12] If *Loving* has not wrought a paradigmatic change in Southern white or national attitudes regarding racial intermarriage, precisely what, then, is the causal significance of *Loving*?

Despite the unchallenged assumption that *Loving* is the primary, if not the exclusive, cause of an increase in interracial marriages, the fact is that we do not know this at all. The only thing we know with some certainty is that there has been an increase in the number of interracially married couples over the decades. While it is certainly easy and convenient to lay that increase at the foot of *Loving,* the presumption should receive as close an interrogation as would any other. Needless to say, this interrogation must be thorough and careful, even though such examination complicates many assertions and assumptions made by proidentity academics. Let me state quite explicitly that I am not questioning the assertion that there has been an increase in marriages between people who believe they are members of different biological racial groups. I do not dispute this particular proposition in any way. What I question is whether those marriages are the direct result of the *Loving* decision, as is so often and so casually maintained by proidentity academics, as opposed to those marriages and indeed *Loving* itself both being aspects of a larger and still-ongoing trend.

For instance, Teresa Williams-León asserts that "in 1967, when the U.S. Supreme Court struck down long-held antimiscegenation laws, the legal marital unions between individuals across racial boundaries became possible."[13] Her statement, however, is not a sensible one, for marital unions across racial boundaries were of course already fully legal in thirty-four other states at the time. Moreover, the states whose existing statutes were invalidated by *Loving* remain the least likely for interracial marriages. A statement such as Williams-León's leaves either an inaccurate impression that no interracial marriages were legal prior to

Loving, or an accurate impression that one is reading less-than-careful writing. In either case, the scholarly integrity of the field of multiracial identity studies is weakened that much more.

Rather than the unproven assertion that *Loving* initiated a paradigm shift in racial behavior, Rachel Moran argues that *Loving* has in fact not drastically changed Americans' behavior in regard to interracial marriage: "Today, *Loving*'s normative ideal of colorblindness in the regulation of marriage is well established. Legal barriers have fallen, but interracial marriages, particularly between blacks and whites, remain an anomaly over thirty years after the decision. Because the Court envisioned race as a biological irrelevancy but was unwilling to coerce intimacy, it has never been clear whether *Loving* succeeded because official behavior changed or whether it failed because marital behavior remains substantially unchanged."[14]

So although the statutes outlawing interracial marriage have been overturned, people's behavior—despite the numbers hoisted up by proidentity academics and activists—has not changed radically, as "the most striking feature of the aftermath of *Loving v. Virginia* is how readily people have accepted segregation in marriage, so long as it is not officially mandated."[15] One might ask how this can be, since everyone, it seems, has presumed the veracity of the *Loving* legend. In fact, there are reasons we may gesture toward, reasons that possess more explanatory power than the mere assertion of the legend itself. According to Moran, "even before *Loving* and perhaps in response to the nascent civil rights movement, the rate of black-white intermarriage increased somewhat between 1950 and 1960 but remained low. After the elimination of laws making miscegenation a crime, the rate of black-white intermarriage rose steadily, although the overall number, about 65,000 couples, stayed small."[16] Moran notes further that such marriages increased to 155,000 in 1982, and 211,000 in 1990.[17] The increase in black/white intermarriage after *Loving* can therefore possibly be seen as a continuation of an already occurring trend.

Beyond this, we must keep in mind that although 211,000 seems like very many more couples than 65,000, the overall population of the United States also increased significantly during those years. Therefore, when people compare the numbers of interracial marriages from, say, 1970 to 1990 or 2000, we will of course see a large increase; however, without a corresponding analysis of the entire country's population change over that same time period—as well as subanalyses of intermarriage by group—no meaning can be assigned to that particular increase in interracial marriages.

Williams-León provides a typical example of this unwarranted presumption when she writes that as a result of *Loving,* "interracial marriages have taken place in larger numbers in the post-civil rights era than in any other time period in U.S. history."[18] Yet her statement is as meaningless as it is sweeping. Of course there have been more interracial marriages since 1967 than in any other period in US history. Mere population growth, improved child mortality rates, advances in healthcare, and increases in immigration would account for that. What may appear to be an obvious and unquestionable deduction is revealed to be far more dubious when subjected to minimal analysis. Yet the number of times *Loving* is invoked by proidentity academics in regard both to interracial marriages and to a supposed biracial baby boom (see below) is astounding in its casualness.

It may well be that rather than a direct relationship with the *Loving* decision, any real increases in interracial marriages are instead attributable to population growth in general, to already existing trends of progression, to more persons living to a marriageable age, and to the positive effects of the civil rights movement in terms of workplace and educational integration. As Moran describes: "Blacks, whether male or female, who marry out are better educated than those who do not. In addition, white men who marry interracially are more likely to have a college education than those who marry within their race. This pattern suggests that integration of higher education and white collar workplaces has produced increasing contact between blacks and whites who are highly educated."[19] *Loving* is convenient, but it is no more likely a direct cause of increased interracial marriages than simple population growth or the integration of workplace and educational institutions. Moreover, when one takes into account the still-prevailing attitudes against intermarriage, particularly in those states whose antimiscegenation statutes were overturned by *Loving,* it becomes even less likely a reason. Instead, far from being the direct cause of some paradigmatic shift, *Loving* is itself an effect of glacially changing racial attitudes. It is the result, not the cause, of a still-ongoing trend in racial adjustment in the United States.

Related to the *Loving* legend, and every bit as unchallenged, is the presumption of a post-*Loving* biracial baby boom. As Moran describes, the children of interracial couples are "sometimes called the 'children of *Loving*'"[20] Again, let us first ensure that proidentity academics are making this claim. Discussing the *Loving* decision, Korgen writes that a "'biracial baby boom' began shortly thereafter."[21] Root informs us that she is seeing young multiracial Americans "grow up in the midst of a 'biracial baby boom.'"[22] Loretta Winters and Herman DeBose indicate that their interest in coauthoring an anthology chapter "was prompted by the biracial 'baby boom' that has occurred since 1967 when the U.S. Supreme Court overturned antimiscegenation laws in 16 states."[23] Williams-León writes of the 1980s as the "period of the 'biracial baby boom.'"[24] Finally, Daniel cites *Loving* as leading to the "birth of 'first-generation' (or biracial) offspring."[25]

It should be clear that, given the claim that these children are the products of interracial marriages resulting directly from the *Loving* decision, every criticism of the *Loving* presumption regarding directly causal increases in interracial marriages works against the presumption of a *Loving*-caused biracial baby boom as well. Clearly, if one cannot establish real evidence of a causal relationship between *Loving* and subsequent increases in interracial marriages, one cannot establish a causal relationship between *Loving* and any children resulting from those same marriages. Lest I be accused here of ignoring the obvious, allow me to insist that, as academics, we should hold firmly to rigorous standards of scholarly investigation and intellectual argument before accepting any thesis, regardless of how obvious or convenient this thesis might seem to some.

I am well aware of the various numbers put forth by academics who make the "*Loving* as cause" presumption; however, the fact is that, absent any evidence beyond the assertion itself, those numbers are just as attributable to the proposition that there was a national thawing of racial attitudes as a result of the successful 1969 *Apollo 11* moon mission, or to the proposition that Americans' racial attitudes melted as a result of the warm feeling with which many may have left theaters after viewing the heartwarming 1967 film *Guess Who's Coming to Dinner.* We will remember as well that interracial marriage was already legal in thirty-four states prior to *Loving,* and that if *Loving* were to indeed have had the direct, watershed effect that has been attributed to it, the sixteen states in which interracial marriage had been illegal previously should have been the primary sources of the subsequent increases. In fact, they should have experienced phenomenally explosive increases. Yet we know this cannot be true, since those states have always been and remain among the lowest in intermarriage rates.

There may indeed exist documentable and incontrovertible proof that the *Loving* decision was the direct cause of increases in interracial marriages and of a biracial baby boom. We may find evidence that in 1968, 1969, 1970, 1971, and 1972, for instance, intermarriage rates in Alabama, Georgia, and Mississippi soared astronomically and continued to soar, and that this was the primary source of the national intermarriage increases pointed to by proidentity academics. I concede fully that this or some other justifying evidence may well be brought to light. My only point is that, to date, it has not been, and that until such time as it is, the presumption for *Loving*-caused intermarriage increases and the presumption for a *Loving*-caused biracial baby boom ought to be treated, by academics at the very least, as the myths they are. I expect proidentity academics to take issue with my arguments here; however, whatever rebuttal may be forthcoming, it simply cannot be a reiteration of the unsupported assertion that interracial marriages and mixed-race births have increased since 1970, and that therefore the direct cause must be the *Loving* decision of 1967. If anything has been demonstrated up to this point, it is the inadequacy of that line of reasoning without any specific and compelling evidence to support it.

But beyond this, there is an even more fundamental criticism of the claims for increases in interracial marriage and for a biracial baby boom. What also works against both presumptions, at least in the black/white case, is the fact that Afro-Americans' historical population mixture problematizes the very notion of interracial marriage and births. It represents an even more fundamental problem than that posed by the "*Loving* as cause" thesis.

Given the extensive population mixture that in many ways defines what it means to be Afro-American, the children who compose the black/white portion of the so-called biracial baby boom cannot in the first place be distinguished in any intellectually responsible way from "regular" Afro-American children. I will return to this point in Chapter 4, but it bears mentioning here as well. Regardless of the misinformation that might be put forth at the level of grassroots activism, are we as scholars truly willing to aver that, to take but one of a multitude of potential examples, a child with one supposedly pure, white-identifying parent and one brown-skinned, black-identifying parent whose mixed ancestry we do not care to acknowledge is somehow *more* multiracial than a child with two light-skinned, black-identifying parents who each have at least one white grandparent? Here, on the issue of interracial marriage and biracial births, is an opportunity to step back and recognize how deeply embedded in the foundation of biological race the claims for interracial marriage and biracial births actually are. It is an opportunity to reject this reification of race, and to reorient the discussion in a more academically defensible direction.

This insistence on facts and on high-quality work is absolutely critical. Unfortunately, without dedicated journals, and without acknowledged academic centers of expertise, scholarly work in the field of multiracial identity studies remains something of a free-for-all. That is why it is essential that those of us who publish work in this subdiscipline and who are claiming it as our own must act to police the field ourselves. In the absence of such self-policing, we run the risk of allowing misinformation and sloppiness to become indistinguishable from good scholarship. When that happens—and as we have seen, it already has happened many times over—all serious scholars with a real interest in the field are the losers.

What I am addressing here is the need for competence, for attention to detail, and for an absolutely uncompromising refusal to accept carelessness and sloppiness. For instance, as I cited above, Korgen writes of the *Loving* decision that a "'biracial baby boom' began shortly thereafter."[26] Korgen's statement meshes nicely with a related comment by Root, who refers to young multiracial people coming of age "when most first-generation mixed-race persons have not been a product of rape, war, or slavery."[27] What unites Korgen's statement and Root's statement is the fact that both assertions are at least three hundred years behind the times.

This is especially disappointing in Korgen's case, as at the cited point in *From Black to Biracial* she has just concluded a historical review based in part on the excellent work of Joel Williamson in his book *New People* (1980).[28] Yet if Korgen has read Williamson carefully, she surely knows that the real biracial baby boom took place in the colonial Chesapeake region, and was characterized by consensual relations between African and Afro-American slave and indentured servant males, and lower-class white females. Considering the historical and cultural importance of what happened in the Chesapeake three hundred years ago, and considering how it and later surges were the source of, as Williamson puts it, "a wellspring of mulattoes, a 'mulatto pool,'" any presumed post-*Loving* biracial baby boom is a comparative drop in the bucket in terms of significance.[29] As I have argued, it is questionable enough to invoke the idea of a post-*Loving* biracial baby boom without evidence, but for Korgen to cite Williamson specifically for historical purposes and to then still evoke the supposed *Loving*–baby boom connection is simply mystifying.

In order for Korgen to propose such a modern biracial baby boom, she must first erase the centuries of race-mixing in the Afro-American population she cites Williamson for, and then recast present-day Afro-Americans as monoracially black.[30] Naomi Pabst locates Korgen's work in *From Black to Biracial* as an "oft-encountered argument within the burgeoning domain of contemporary critical mixed-race studies," an argument asserting that "black/white biracial subjects used to be automatically and unproblematically classified as black but should now increasingly be considered fundamentally mixed."[31] According to Pabst, "The downside of this thesis is that it oversimplifies blackness and mixedness, respectively and interrelatedly, as once straightforward and solidified and now complex and contested, when the latter has been the case all along."[32] I will have more to say about this particular brand of historical revisionism, and the threat it poses, in Chapter 4.

We see a similar kind of ahistoricism in Root's above-quoted claim that the present age is one in which "most first-generation mixed-race persons have not been a product of rape, war, or slavery." I take her meaning here to be that in past ages most first-generation mixed-race persons were in fact products of rape, war, or slavery. In the US context, at least, I question Root's formulation, as it is another one of those convenient and obvious-sounding statements that too often go unchallenged. Afro-Americans constitute one of the largest mixed-race groups in the United States, so Root's statement should certainly apply to this group, but does it? Do we know that there has ever been a period of British North American or US history in which most first-generation black/white persons were the products of rape, war, or slavery?

The answer is that we do not know any such thing. As Williamson's historical overview demonstrates, the initial large mass of mulattoes hailed from consensual relations in the colonial Chesapeake.[33] Consensual relations had always been ongoing, both Northern and Southern, and we have no way of knowing the gross numbers of how many black/white children were born as a result of white (or African or Afro-American) rape versus as a result of consensual relations. We simply have no idea. Am I denying here that female slaves were raped by white owners, owners' sons, and overseers? Certainly not. I am merely pointing out that we have no idea at all how often slave-rape by whites took place, how often it led to children being born alive, and—most important in the present context—if it happened more often than consensual sexual relations leading to black/white births. Root's statement sounds obvious but is in fact insupportable, as her claim rests on data that we will simply never have access to.

In that sense it is similar to Root's also good-sounding but just as unverifiable claim that "for most of America's history, mixed-race children were shunned, but over time their situation has improved."[34] Again, where are the data that can support this emotion-laden assertion? This is not to suggest that mixed-race children have not suffered over the years, but precisely what Root is intending to get at here is not at all clear. If mixed-race children were shunned for "most of America's history," in what years were they shunned and in what years were they not? Were they shunned any more than were overweight, disabled, Jewish, Irish-descended, or southern European–descended children? Whom is Root suggesting as having been the agent or agents of shunning—the federal government, individual citizens, family members? The answers to these questions would make a great difference to any analysis of her claim.

Root's ahistoricism continues, albeit in a relatively more recent vein, when she avers that "it was rarely challenged only a generation ago that white men could produce white babies only with white women; white women can produce any-race babies; but only white women can produce white babies; black women can only have black babies; women of color produce babies of color and never white babies; men of color produce babies of color and never white babies; and black men can produce only black babies."[35] It hardly bears pointing out that every one of these propositions remains completely unchallenged today.

One might object that I am overreacting to what merely are harmless comments by Root—that she either miswrote or was not intending to be subjected to this level of scrutiny. But that is precisely the problem with so much proidentity academic writing. Proidentity academics seem always to be miswriting or to be writing in ways that do not withstand even minimal challenge. Emotion, bathos, and, frankly, overt cheerleading seem often to overwhelm all sense of objectivity or concern for historical accuracy and logically valid argumentation. The result of each unchallenged assertion is yet another addition to a mountain of misinformation that grows ever larger and ever more solidified, much like the effect of water dripping on a stalagmite. And when, through lack of critical analysis and scholarly refutation, that misinformation is allowed to become *information,* the corrective task is thereby made doubly hard. It is in this context that I find myself arguing that, generally speaking, there is in fact no such thing as a first-generation black/white person, but this discussion, because of where it will lead us, will have to wait until Chapter 4.

I turn now to interrogating the assertion or assumption that multiracial identity—specifically, black/white multiracial identity—has undergone a paradigm shift such that black/white persons of the post-*Loving* era now "correctly" identify themselves as multiracial at a significantly higher rate than do those of prior generations. This inquiry is completely independent of the question of whether *Loving* did or did not have the attitude-changing effect attributed to it by multiracial identity advocates.

Thus I will point to *Loving* only as a temporal reference mark. Regardless of what *Loving* is or is not responsible for directly, I want to assess the claim that a new multiracial ideology has taken hold such that today's black/white children and young adults are "correctly" identifying as multiracial, whereas their pre–mid-1960s counterparts were "incorrectly" identifying as black. The reader will recall that this was a conclusion reached specifically by each of the three authors I highlighted in Chapter 1—Brown, Kilson, and Korgen. I would suggest instead that black/white children have been *indoctrinated* toward a multiracial identity at a higher rate since 1967 than was the case prior to that year, and that white mothers have had something significant to do with this.

I want to be absolutely clear that I am not questioning the assertion that the post-*Loving* generation consists of a relatively higher percentage of people who think they represent the combined essences of two different biological racial groups—who in other words think they are biologically multiracial. I do not doubt this phenomenon at all. What I question is precisely what this phenomenon means in terms of "progress," and in terms of the supposed "correctness" of any particular racial identity, including black/white multiracial identity. As I have begun to argue, I do not—as do the writers I have mentioned previously—attribute this shift to a supposed post-*Loving* freedom to "correctly" identify as multiracial, but rather to explicit indoctrination to identify as such.

As I have indicated in earlier chapters, there are some topics that have been subject to far too much politeness within the scholarly discourse of multiracial identity studies. The silence on these topics has led to serious problems in being able to discuss adequately all factors relating to the study of multiracial identity. I suggest that we ought to open one of those closed topics by evaluating the motivations of some white mothers who take part in the indoctrination of their black/white children toward a multiracial identity. I would not go so far as Jon Spencer, who, in criticizing two formerly prominent multiracial activists (one a white mother, the other a Hispanic male), writes that "the point is not simply how many blacks would rather identify as multiracial, but that multiracialists such as [Susan] Graham and [Carlos] Fernandez, who are not black, are tampering with the naming and characterization of black people."[36] However, there is a need to at least acknowledge and to come to grips with some of the more questionable motivations operating in this matter.

It seems to me that white mothers especially have taken the lead in carrying out the indoctrination to which I have been referring, many of them out of some impulse—frankly, a rather selfish one—to be acknowledged as part of their children's heritage. While this may sound like something of a harsh criticism to levy against mothers, I shall justify it in what follows. This desire for explicit recognition provides the opportunity for interesting philosophical exploration. At the very least, these white mothers appear to be asserting a demand for their own visibility in or through their children. Apparently, it is not satisfying enough for them to enjoy possession of their own white identities—the typically nonracialized and most privileged identity in the United States—but they desire to stake a claim to a portion of their children's identities as well. As Laurie Mengel puts it, "rather than attempting to understand and address the complexities of ethnic identity for mixed race people, many White parents imposed their choices of identification on their multiracial children."[37] In the cases of black/white children, most of these white parents are mothers.

In a typical example, one white mother puts her support of federally recognized multiracial identity this way: "There may be some parents who like the multiracial idea because they want their children to be better than black, but there are also plenty like me who just want to be acknowledged. I'm part of this kid, too, no matter who he looks like."[38] It is a fair question to interrogate this motivation, however. Precisely who are multiracial identity and the multiracial identity movement for— are they for the benefit of mixed-race children and adults, or are they instead for the benefit of their white parents? Who is the movement composed of chiefly?

In Tanya Hernández' view, "the principal proponents of the multiracial category are 'monoracial' Black and White parents of biracial children."[39] Kim Williams provides the following analysis of the multiracial identity movement: "Ironically, and in spite of the fact that multiracial leaders *say* that multiracial identity is constitutive of people across all racial mixes, there are not very many multiracial adults involved in the Multiracial Movement. This is largely an effort of monoracially identified parents *on behalf of their children*. . . . And so, we end up with the compelling fact that most multiracial organizations are in fact run by white, middle-class women living in suburbs."[40] Heather Dalmage makes a similar point when describing an organization joined by a white mother whom she interviewed: "Like other multiracial family organizations, this one is disproportionately comprised of white mothers of multiracial children."[41]

Finally, Rebecca King-O'Riain, considering the influence of parents on the construction of multiracial discourses, notes that "in the Multiracial Movement, this has taken the form of the overrepresentation of white mothers on the forefront of activism on behalf of their multiracial children."[42] Moreover, King-O'Riain continues, "many of the founders of HIF [Hapa Issues Forum, an Asian/Pacific Islander multiracial organization] explained to me that they did not feel comfortable in multiracial organizations dominated by black/white multiracial family members and issues."[43] Given that white mothers of black/white children are the most vocal component in such organizations, it is not difficult to surmise the source of the discomfort felt by the HIF founders. In this light it is also not surprising that three of the most recent single-authored scholarly books in favor of black/white multiracial identity have been written by white women academics, two of whom are mothers of black/white children, and the other of whom is an aunt of a black/white child.

The impact of white mothers on the movement for recognition of multiracial identity, federal or otherwise, should not be understated. It is important to assess and to understand the relationship between post-*Loving* white mothers and the identity choices, if they are indeed choices, of their black/white offspring. Much has been made of Afro-American investment in hypodescent, and of the pressure that Afro-American family members, friends, acquaintances, and even strangers exert on black/white persons to identify as black. To the extent that this has happened and continues to happen, it should be recognized as indoctrination and should be problematized. In fact, multiracial activists and academics often deride the argument for monoracial black identification of black/white individuals as being not only a retrograde form of indoctrination but a psychologically damaging one as well.

However, indoctrination that moves in a different direction, in the direction of multiracial identity, not only fails to be at all problematized but also is in fact celebrated. Or to be more precise, the ultimate *effect* of that indoctrination—the parental placement of multiracial identity on children (for I think we err seriously to call it "choosing")—is celebrated as a psychosocio breakthrough of the highest order. Yet indoctrination is indoctrination, is it not? How is teaching children that they are multiracial any less indoctrinating than teaching them that they are black? Unless we can determine that one or the other of these two modes of indoctrination is "correct"—and such a determination will certainly not be forthcoming, since what we are addressing here, after all, is personal identity based on the nonsense of biological race—both forms of indoctrination should be condemned with equal vigor. To those who would counter that this is an impractical position to take in a nation obsessed with race, I reply that those of us who are aware of race's falsity ought to condemn the continuing assignation of racial identities, including multiracial identities. Either we believe in biological race or we do not, and if we do not we should act accordingly.[44] Sadly, but hardly surprisingly, this is not the case among either activists or proidentity academics.

Instead, we find an assent to race, and a single-minded pursuit of a separate multiracial identity. Of the four different identity options Kerry Ann Rockquemore has determined to be utilized by black/white persons, she finds what she calls the "protean" identity to be "an ideal example of the way in which race, and therefore racial categorizations, are fluid due to their social construction."[45] With the protean identity, "individuals may move fluidly among black, white, and/or multiracial identities, using whichever identity may be situationally appropriate for a specific interactional context."[46] This identity option would seem to be a perfect example of an identity that "delegitimizes both the existence of mutual exclusivity between races and the biological reality of racial categories," both of which are principles that activist white mothers have long claimed to drive their refusal to accept monoracial identification for their children.[47] "Strangely, however," as Rockquemore reports, "this identity option is neither accepted nor promoted by the Multiracial Movement."[48]

There are some white mothers who are willing to subordinate themselves and any purely personal interests long enough to engage in real activism, however. Dalmage writes that those who "were willing to question racial identities and reach across the color line for connection and understanding were less likely to advocate for a multiracial category, and spent more time in black organizations and communities than multiracial organizations. The voices of white multiracial family members who are struggling from *within* communities of color are often silenced, marginalized, and dismissed by the more vocal advocates for a multiracial category and color-blind agenda."[49] This bias is one that is shared by activists and proidentity academics alike.

Korgen makes an extraordinarily telling, albeit unrealized, point when she writes that black/white children "who are raised in poor, predominantly minority neighborhoods by parents who urge them to recognize only their black background will most likely believe they have no real choice in their racial definition."[50] Her statement is astonishing because it makes precisely the opposite point than she intends, and serves to illustrate the tremendous bias on the proidentity academic front. What choice do any children have who are indoctrinated by their parents to identify a certain way? What is the difference between such a case as cited by Korgen and its opposite? In other words, I can just as easily assert that black/white children who are raised in middle-class, predominantly white neighborhoods by parents who urge them to identify as multiracial will most likely believe they have no real choice in their racial definition. They would have just as difficult a time resisting their parents' efforts at indoctrinating them to a multiracial identity as the hypothetical children in Korgen's example would have in resisting their parents' efforts at indoctrinating them to a black identity. The point Korgen actually makes is that all indoctrination involves the denial of choice on the part of the indoctrinated.

Yet to suggest that some white mothers are indoctrinating their black/white children is sure to bring gasps of shock, when in fact there is absolutely no structural distinction between that form of indoctrination and the black indoctrination decried so stridently by proidentity activists and academics. I can relate an example from my own personal experience that will be very relevant here. On October 27, 1999, I gave a public lecture at the Winchester Community Center in Las Vegas, Nevada. The presentation was titled "Race in the Twenty First Century" and centered on a newly published book of mine on the subject of multiracial identity.[51] During the question and answer session following the formal presentation, an older couple identified themselves as the parents of Susan Graham, the executive director of Project RACE (Reclassify All Children Equally), at the time an important national multiracial advocacy organization. I remember very distinctly that during a discussion with this older couple of the racial identity of Graham's son, Ryan, the man (Ryan's grandfather) volunteered that Ryan's mother (Susan) had indoctrinated Ryan toward a multiracial identity. At this, the woman (Ryan's grandmother) interjected, "Don't say 'indoctrinated.'" I can think of no better symbolic exclamation point for my argument.

A white mother makes her own motivations plain when she asks in reference to her multiracial children: "Why do I have to call them black . . . ? Then I don't get my ethn-, they don't carry my identity."[52] Generally speaking, up to this point writers and commentators have exhibited excessive politeness in not taking these sorts of attitudes to task when analyzing the multiracial movement in the United States, but clearly the attitudes of white mothers should be every bit as open to scrutiny as the supposed new-generation enlightenment of their multiracially identifying children. Mengel does offer a critique, however, and describes one particular example this way: "One Black/White woman remembered finding a positive racial identity through James Brown's song 'Say it Loud, I'm Black and I'm Proud.' Her White mother revealed her own self-absorption with regard to her daughter's racial identity by reprimanding, 'Why do you have to refer to yourself that way? Calling yourself black makes me feel like I'm invisible. Like I don't exist. Like I don't count.'"[53] In Mengel's view, "the mother here appears to be more concerned with her inclusion in her daughter's identity, than in the evolution of her daughter's identity, or her daughter's understanding of race in a racist society."[54]

Reginald Robinson, writing from the position that the Multiracial Category Movement (MCM) "constitutes a radical shift in our racial consciousness," asks, "Does it quite frankly matter that white mothers for example are key proponents of the MCM? Does it also matter that these white mothers might be motivated by a desire to be validated in their children's identity? Does it matter to the MCM that these white mothers find traditional racial categories too constraining, too marginalizing? Basically, does it matter that the white mothers are narrowly driven by selfish motives?"[55]

I answer that, yes, indeed it does matter. It matters because not only are these mothers adding to the madness over biological race in the United States, but they are also helping to institute a false split (see Chapter 4) between Americans of sub-Saharan African and European descent—a split that privileges only the children that they attempt to bestow the benefits of their whiteness upon. To the degree that these mothers' children are elevated by that association with whiteness, "regular" Afro-American children (who possess just as much population mixture in their ancestries) are disadvantaged. Adding selfish motives to this already alarming situation serves only to make it that much worse.

Some may be uncomfortable with the trajectory of this discussion, in which I have striven to point out the significant impact of white mothers on their black/white children's identities. However, I am merely illustrating and providing evidence for what proidentity academics have themselves been arguing—that since the mid-1960s white mothers have taken on a much more aggressive role in determining their black/white children's identities. This is the essence of what is distilled from both the *Loving* and the biracial baby boom legends. Regardless of the mythical status of either proposition, proidentity academics have been arguing that this alleged paradigm shift in racial identification (although we know from Chapter 1 that such a change has not been shown to be representative of the broader population of black/white multiracials of the same age) is a result of parents becoming more involved in the process of instilling a multiracial identity. Moreover, whenever one reads interview studies of black/white children or their parents, a particular pattern usually emerges in which Afro-American fathers are either noncommittal or stress the need for a black identity based on the reality of the racist system in which we all live, while white mothers are always the more aggressive parties in advocating the adoption of a multiracial identity for their children. I would be very surprised to find proidentity academics disagreeing with this point.

Consider the words of yet another white mother: "I was bound and determined that my child would not be raised black, would not be called black, because I'm white and half of her background is white."[56] I wonder if this mother would be so very much against the reverse case. In other words, would she demonstrate as much animosity toward her child being raised as white, assuming the child's phenotype would allow it? Rarely in either the activist or the proidentity academic literature do we find the more rational view (in my opinion) as expressed by the following white mother: "They know who their mother is. They know what their family history is . . . and so I never felt like I've heard other white women say they felt like they were left out or something. I never felt that."[57] Finally, a last comment gets at the underlying anger that I think is foundational in these cases: "It seems to me that to merely label her 'black' is not an accurate reflection of her true identity and it angers me that my own heritage is blotted out in society's view of my daughter's background."[58] Beyond its bizarreness and selfishness, this sort of matricolonial project points out the extent to which biological race is hopelessly intertwined with the multiracial idea, as this mother strives to imprint her own whiteness, one way or another, on her daughter.

During the 1990s one often heard this "denial of existence" myth being raised by multiracial identity activists, white mothers in particular, as a justification for instituting a federal multiracial category. The argument stated that white parents were effectively erased from existence without such a category at the federal level. One did not expect the nonscholar activists who raised this argument to actually support it with evidence, and of course they did not. However, as with other facets of the old activist program, today's pro–multiracial identity academics have revivified the myth essentially word-for-word. They have also maintained the tradition of providing no evidence for this claim, as when Brown endorses the notion of denial of existence in writing that some "white parents may want to validate their biological and psychological connection to the child, which is wiped out with the provision of a black label."[59]

As I have done previously, it is necessary once again to interrogate closely what is essentially either an incredibly careless or an incredibly outlandish assertion (or both). Brown is actually arguing here that a parent's most basic connection to the child will be severed if the child does not assume a multiracial identity. Yet how can a biological connection be "wiped out"? Is Brown suggesting that the child thereby changes physically and becomes monoracially black in a scientific, genetic way? Assuming that she is being a careful and serious scholar, what else could she possibly mean? Moreover, how can a psychological connection be "wiped out"? What does this particular admonition even mean?

This is a hefty warning given by Brown, and if true it speaks of extraordinarily dire consequences for both parent and child. Is the mother no longer really the child's mother? Would Brown actually feel that, as a mother, she had neither a biological nor a psychological connection to her own children had she not indoctrinated them toward a multiracial identity? Nor do I take her above-cited statement to have been a mere slip, as a few pages later Brown advises that some white parents "may be reluctant to provide a racial label that denies their parenthood and existence."[60] Now, it would be far less problematic had Brown written that some white parents may be reluctant to provide a racial label that *they think* denies their parenthood and existence, but that is not what she wrote. Brown's words state in quite a clear way that in her view the wrong racial label actually "denies their parenthood and existence." Again, how sensible a statement is this, and is it academically incompetent or merely unacceptably careless?

It is a very, very serious problem when academics who apparently do not respect the field of multiracial identity studies feel that they can simply meander in and publish careless work merely because they have mixed-race children or other relatives. A psychologist writing in a purportedly scholarly book on multiracial identity that a particular racial label may result in the "wiping out" of a mother's "biological and psychological connection" to her child—no matter how ridiculous a statement this actually is—will unfortunately be taken seriously by many people who read it. The result is significant misinformation on the one hand, and scholarly derision for the academic integrity of the field on the other.

Some readers will no doubt question the vigor of my criticism of pro–multiracial identity academics, including this current instance. My response is that someone has to stand up and refuse to allow poor-quality academic work to pass by without challenge. The fact is that Brown's claim that a "black label" will wipe out a white mother's biological and psychological connection to her child is a patently ridiculous assertion, particularly so when presented by an academic in a scholarly book. It is

not acceptable, and should not be accepted. This is not about mere difference of opinion, which is all part of scholarly discourse; it is about
the propagation of pure nonsense dressed as academic research. What is
published matters, what is printed makes a difference, and what is
allowed to become part of the field's discourse is critical. What some
might see as an impolite breach of academic etiquette on my part, I see
instead as an absolutely essential defense of the need for scholarly
integrity, let the chips fall where they may.

Indeed, the stakes involved here are far higher than demure concerns about politeness or tact, as the misinformation propagated by academics writing in support of black/white multiracial identity, in addition
to muddying the philosophical waters, has an important practical consequence. Whether purposeful or not, scholarly support for black/white
multiracial identity—especially so-called first-generation identity—
threatens to facilitate an ominous change to the already flawed and
already problematic racial paradigm in the United States. In Chapter 4,
we will examine how this paradigm may be heading from bad to even
worse for one particular group of long-suffering Americans.

Notes

1. Ray Bradbury, *The Martian Chronicles* (New York: Bantam, 1979),
130.
2. Ursula Brown, *The Interracial Experience: Growing Up Black/White
Racially Mixed in the United States* (Westport: Praeger, 2001), 18–19.
3. G. Reginald Daniel, *More Than Black? Multiracial Identity and the
New Racial Order* (Philadelphia: Temple University Press, 2002), 6.
4. Ibid., 116.
5. Kathleen Korgen, *From Black to Biracial: Transforming Racial
Identity Among Americans* (Westport: Praeger, 1999), 20.
6. Rachel Moran, *Interracial Intimacy: The Regulation of Race &
Romance* (Chicago: University of Chicago Press, 2001), 102.
7. Ibid., 105, 107.
8. Renee C. Romano, *Race Mixing: Black-White Marriage in Postwar
America* (Cambridge: Harvard University Press, 2003), 253.
9. Ibid.
10. Gunnar Myrdal, *An American Dilemma: The Negro Problem and
Modern Democracy* (New York: Harper and Brothers, 1944), 60–61.
11. Ibid., 60.
12. Romano, *Race Mixing,* 253.
13. Teresa Williams-León, "Check All That Apply: Trends and Prospectives Among Asian-Descent Multiracials," in *New Faces in a Changing
America: Multiracial Identity in the 21st Century,* eds. Loretta Winters and
Herman DeBose (Thousand Oaks, CA: Sage, 2003), 160.

14. Moran, *Interracial Intimacy,* 101.

15. Ibid., 124.

16. Ibid., 103.

17. Ibid.

18. Williams-León, "Check All That Apply," 160–161.

19. Moran, *Interracial Intimacy,* 103. While acknowledging the possible effect of workplace and educational integration, it must be noted that this in no way justifies the outrageously unrepresentative interview samples compiled by Kilson and Korgen (see Chapter 1).

20. Moran, *Interracial Intimacy,* 9.

21. Korgen, *From Black to Biracial,* 20.

22. Maria P. P. Root, "Five Mixed-Race Identities: From Relic to Revolution," in *New Faces in a Changing America,* eds. Winters and DeBose, 10.

23. Loretta Winters and Herman DeBose, "The Dilemma of Biracial People of African American Descent," in *New Faces in a Changing America,* eds. Winters and DeBose, 127.

24. Williams-León, "Check All That Apply," 161.

25. Daniel, *More Than Black?* 6.

26. Korgen, *From Black to Biracial,* 20.

27. Root, "Five Mixed-Race Identities," 4.

28. Joel Williamson, *New People: Miscegenation and Mulattoes in the United States* (New York: Free Press, 1980).

29. Ibid., 57.

30. Korgen, *From Black to Biracial,* 15–17.

31. Naomi Pabst, "Blackness/Mixedness: Contestations over Crossing Signs," *Cultural Critique* 54 (Spring 2003): 180.

32. Ibid.

33. Williamson, *New People,* chap. 1.

34. Maria P. P. Root, *Love's Revolution: Interracial Marriage* (Philadelphia: Temple University Press, 2001), 136.

35. Ibid., 145.

36. Jon M. Spencer, *The New Colored People: The Mixed-Race Movement in America* (New York: New York University Press, 1997), 64.

37. Laurie M. Mengel, "Triples—The Social Evolution of a Multiracial Panethnicity: An Asian American Perspective," in *Rethinking "Mixed Race,"* eds. David Parker and Miri Song (London: Pluto, 2001), 105.

38. Quoted in Linda Mathews, "More Than Identity Rides on a New Racial Category," *New York Times,* July 6, 1996, A7.

39. Tanya K. Hernández, "'Multiracial' Discourse: Racial Classifications in an Era of Color-Blind Jurisprudence," *Maryland Law Review* 57, no. 97 (1998): 106.

40. Kim Williams, "Linking the Civil Rights and Multiracial Movements," in *The Politics of Multiracialism: Challenging Racial Thinking,* ed. Heather M. Dalmage (Albany: State University of New York Press, 2004), 90.

41. Heather M. Dalmage, "Protecting Racial Comfort, Protecting White Privilege," in *The Politics of Multiracialism,* ed. Dalmage, 206.

42. Rebecca Chiyoko King-O'Riain, "Model Majority? The Struggle for Identity Among Multiracial Japanese Americans," in *The Politics of Multiracialism,* ed. Dalmage, 184.

43. Ibid., 185.

44. I am referring here to personal identity, which is a different issue than the question of whether we should do away with federal racial statistics. Until we develop an alternative but still-effective means of monitoring continuing racial discrimination, federal racial statistics remain our best weapon in the battle against racism, particularly institutional racism.

45. Kerry Ann Rockquemore, "Deconstructing Tiger Woods: The Promise and the Pitfalls of Multiracial Identity," in *The Politics of Multiracialism,* ed. Dalmage, 130.

46. Ibid., 129.

47. Ibid., 130.

48. Ibid.

49. Dalmage, "Protecting Racial Comfort," 216.

50. Korgen, *From Black to Biracial,* 84.

51. Rainier Spencer, *Spurious Issues: Race and Multiracial Identity Politics in the United States* (Boulder: Westview, 1999).

52. Quoted in Paul C. Rosenblatt, Terry A. Karis, and Richard Powell, *Multiracial Couples: Black & White Voices* (Thousand Oaks, CA: Sage, 1995), 202.

53. Mengel, "Triples," 105.

54. Ibid.

55. Reginald L. Robinson, "The Shifting Race-Consciousness Matrix and the Multiracial Category Movement: A Critical Reply to Professor Hernández," *Boston College Third World Law Journal* 20, no. 2 (Spring 2000): 274.

56. Quoted in Romano, *Race Mixing,* 280.

57. Quoted in Rosenblatt, Karis, and Powell, *Multiracial Couples,* 210.

58. Quoted in Moran, *Interracial Intimacy,* 156.

59. Brown, *The Interracial Experience,* 65.

60. Ibid., 70.

4

Distinction Without Difference: The Insidious Argument for First-Generation Black/White Multiracial Identity

*Herskovits and other researchers as well combined the physical exami-
nation of their subjects with questions concerning racial background.
The answers to these questions produced very interesting indexes into
the nature of miscegenation, past and present. Herskovits found that
71.7 percent of his subjects were of mixed white and black ancestry and,
further, that more than a quarter, 27.3 percent, claimed Indian heritage
as well. Only 22 percent were black. His findings seemed accurate
enough for such samples as he used and reinforced the conclusion of the
Census Bureau in 1918 that roughly three-quarters of the Negro population was mixed black and white. Also it was not greatly surprising that
many Negroes were part Indian in view of the facts that the mixture had
begun so early and diffusion was always a function of time.*

—Joel Williamson, *New People*[1]

*"Everybody's trying to claim something special in their background—
a Scottish grandfather, a Native American grandmother. But the M.N.
[Mulatto Nation] is trying to keep it to first-generation mixtures, you
know."*

—Danzy Senna, "The Mulatto Millennium"[2]

Many, many people of combined European and sub-Saharan African
ancestry have lived and died in British North America and the
United States over the past nearly four hundred years. These people have
had all variations of mixture—some fifty/fifty, some eighty/twenty, some
twenty/eighty. These shores have at some place and at some time likely
seen nearly every possibility of mixture between the two, resulting in a
large and genetically diverse subsection of the populace. In the United
States today, we know these people as the Afro-American population,
although the number includes a great many unknown whites as well.[3]

Many generations of mixed-ancestry Afro-Americans have come and gone in the past four centuries. Some of them were acutely aware of their mixed ancestry, some knew they had a quantity of European ancestry somewhere, and others neither knew nor cared about it at all. What they all shared and what they share with those who are of mixed ancestry today is a predicate (in many ways inconsequential and even meaningless)—being, popularly speaking, "racially mixed." At some point long ago it actually did fail to matter, as from that point onward, with the exception of recent sub-Saharan African, and possibly Caribbean, immigrants, all so-called blacks in the United States have been racially mixed whether they or anyone else realized it or not.[4] And this is the important point—one either does or does not have population mixture in one's ancestry. For thirty million people, it is not a question of choosing to have that particular ancestral mixture, for it is already there.

By stating that the phenomenon of sub-Saharan African–European population mixture failed to matter at some point long ago, I mean so in a purely logical sense, of course. For many decades and possibly for centuries, all Afro-Americans (with the above caveat about recent immigrants) have had some European ancestry, and so to say "mixed-race Afro-Americans" is to engage in a certain degree of redundancy. It is in this vein that Jayne Ifekwunigwe reminds us that "these heralded acts of so-called transracial transgression actually transpired long before they were re-invented by the American (and British) media. And this very old story continues."[5] Nonetheless, it has mattered tremendously, although sadly and pointlessly, for many people through the centuries, and it continues to matter to a portion of the population today. The reason for this is that many people persist in believing in the fallacy of race. The unfortunate fact is that far too large a number of Americans believe in biological race, including many academics who claim that they do not.

Indeed, academics appearing to deny biological race by substituting social race in its place are among the greatest purveyors of the fallacy. Social race, socially defined race, race as socially determined, race as socially designated, or race as a social reality are all the same thing—evasive means used by certain academics (particularly sociologists) to make biological race central to their scholarly work. They do this by denying biological race on the surface, and then deploying one of the varieties of social race in its place with no real difference between the two.[6] In short, any academic who classifies as multiracial the child of a socially defined black parent and a socially defined white parent *because* that child is the biological offspring of those two parents, is an academic who is invested fully in the fallacy of biological race, all appeals to social race notwithstanding.

There are several related phenomena that come together and intertwine to construct or create the subject of this chapter—first-generation black/white multiracial identity. The first phenomenon is the belief in biological race that so many Americans still share, a good many academics included. The second phenomenon is an absolute refusal to problematize, interrogate, or otherwise question the pure status of whiteness. Whiteness is crucial to the maintenance of hypodescent—that supposed bane of multiracial identity advocates—but in a most ironic (or hypocritical) way the proponents of multiracial identity, through their deployment of a selective hypodescent, do every bit as much as Afro-Americans to perpetuate the hypodescent myth. This leads to the third phenomenon, which involves the erasure and re-creation of black Americans. It is in fact yet another abuse of Afro-Americans, another instance of them being forced to serve white interests in this country. Kathleen Korgen has it exactly backward in the title of her book *From Black to Biracial* (1999).[7] The true trajectory of blackness, if you will, in regard to the multiracial identity movement, is not from black to biracial, but rather and most decidedly from biracial to black. By this I mean that multiracial black/white Americans (i.e., all Afro-Americans) have their pasts erased and are thereby re-created as monoracially black so that they may stand ready to be posited as parents of multiracial children should they procreate with whites.

In a very important way the movement for black/white multiracial identity involves the creation of two groups of people—multiracial children as well as the monoracially black halves of their respective parent sets. And for every monoracially black parent who is thereby created, an Afro-American parent is erased. By necessity as well, this means that the generations and generations of Afro-Americans I began this chapter by describing are also erased, since every Afro-American, living and dead, is potentially the parent of a black/white child. It is within the realm of that potentiality that the erasure takes place. The erasure is accomplished very quietly and very neatly, but it is an erasure nonetheless—of hundreds of years of history, of life stories, of realities. It is important to acknowledge that those realities are erased explicitly for the sake of erecting the mirage of modern-day multiracial identity. It is an axiological shifting, a reordering of positive value from that which exists to that which does not, and the concomitant extirpation of the former. In that sense it is also a kind of robbery.

How is all this accomplished? As I mentioned in Chapter 1 and will reflect on again here, the idea of multiracial identity depends absolutely on biological race. There cannot even be a conception of multiracial identity absent the clear and unequivocal acceptance of biological race. After all, we are talking about the biological offspring of (allegedly) differently raced parents. As we have seen, dressing biological race in the disguise of social race is a mere obfuscation for sociologists and psychologists that allows them to appear to deny race while clinging to it ever more tightly and ever more obscenely. We should not underestimate the boost given by proidentity academics to the growing fallacy of first-generation black/white multiracial identity. Through biased research (Chapter 1), through generally poor-quality academic work (Chapter 2), and by resurrecting the sievelike arguments of activists in the 1990s (Chapter 3), today's proidentity academics are facilitating the first-generation illusion by a significant degree.

So, beginning with a firm belief in biological race, and abetted by academics providing what appears at first glance to be legitimate scholarly support, we are witness to an attempted sleight of hand that is singularly notable for its obvious transparency. To wit, a white person whose racial purity is never questioned is posited as one parent, and a black person whose mixed ancestry is never considered is posited as the other parent. (We may or may not be presented with the equivocation that the races of these parents are socially determined or socially defined, as that depends upon the sophistication of the person describing the scenario.) The alchemical result is that any children this couple may conceive together are determined to be first-generation black/white multiracials.

The critical point is that the race of such children is not socially determined or socially defined, as such definition—aside from being consistent logically with the way the parents' races are socially determined or socially defined—would lead to an outcome not favored by multiracial advocates. Namely, it would likely lead to the children being socially defined as black via the despised mechanism of hypodescent. Rather, the racial identity of such children is biologically determined. They need nothing else but to be known as the biological children of their socially defined parents in order for the multiracial label to be affixed. Here we see a major inconsistency of multiracial advocacy— what is for the lack of a better term a bait-and-switch—for the racial criterion is thereby switched invalidly from social designation to biology in the cases of supposed first-generation children. If one accepts that such children are first-generation black/white multiracials because they are the biological children of these socially defined parents, then it simply must be that one has thereby replaced those parents' social designations of race with biological designations. Anything else would be not only hypocritical and inconsistent, but also an abomination of the gift of logical thought.

In order to better see the workings of this social-to-biological conversion, let us more closely examine our parent couple, whom we will designate as consisting of a white mother and a black father. What is our white mother's racial ancestry, her personal history of population mixture? She might be able to trace her presumed lineage back a thousand years or perhaps only two generations. I refer to her lineage as "presumed" because, regardless of the documents we might possess or the family trees we might construct, no one can be truly sure of the accuracy (or the purity) of one's lineage, not even to the most recent generations. At any rate, it does not really matter, as no one will interrogate, problematize, or otherwise question the purity of her whiteness. In fact, it is absolutely essential that no challenge whatsoever be made regarding her racial purity. Multiracial identity advocates (scholars and nonscholars alike) see her as a woman of pure white racial identity who, when procreating with a black male, can produce multiracial children. In this way, the US racial paradigm remains unchallenged, the nonsense of biological race remains unchallenged, and the central pillar of hypodescent—white racial purity—remains unchallenged.

The other half of our parent set is a black male, and with him something of an opposite phenomenon takes place. His white mate's racial purity is not problematized because it matters very much that it not be challenged. His own racial purity, however, is not problematized precisely because it does not matter at all. His mixed ancestry of European and sub-Saharan African population groups (and likely Native American as well) is irrelevant to his re-created monoracial black identity. It is in this sense that his old reality of being of mixed ancestry is erased, and his new identity of simply being black is created. This happens all the time, but most especially when a particular birth must be validated as being multiracial. Mixed-race Afro-Americans (a deliberate and acknowledged redundancy here for the purpose of making a point) are continually being erased and re-created as monoracially black in order to further the myth of hypodescent and the fallacy of biological race that supports it. In this way, advocates of first-generation black/white multiracial identity are the real purveyors of hypodescent. Moreover, they are the true hypodescent experts as they employ hypodescent in a selective fashion, as opposed to the simpler and cruder blanket manner.

Black/white multiracial identity advocates claim to despise the US tradition of hypodescent, but on closer inspection of actual practice their opprobrium is revealed to be of a highly discriminating order. This is so because they do not condemn every instance of the application of hypodescent; rather, they condemn only those instances that would complicate their desire to create multiracial children. When hypodescent facilitates multiracial births, they are all for it. In our example, multiracial identity advocates are well aware that the father, being Afro-American, is among the most genetically mixed people in the country. They are well aware that unless he or his parents are recent immigrants from sub-Saharan Africa, or possibly the Caribbean, he undoubtedly has European ancestry. They are well aware that there is no such thing as a purely black Afro-American. Yet in spite of all of this, they impose hypodescent upon him and re-create him as monoracially black in a kind of racial retrofitting.

Activist white mothers are completely unconcerned about the hypodescent that makes their Afro-American husbands black; they are concerned only about the hypodescent that would render their children black, as activist white mother and Project RACE executive director Susan Graham illustrates: "My husband, who is Black, went to our local Recreation and Parks Department to enroll our five-year-old daughter in a gymnastics program. . . . Our daughter was not with him. A clerk checked off 'Black' [on the registration form]. In other words, the clerk looked at the father and made the assumption that the child was Black. . . . The point is: she was mistaken. My husband has a Multiracial child and the clerk had no way of knowing. . . . The problem here is . . . the old rule of hypo-descent."[8]

Notice that on the one hand Graham embraces readily the hypodescent that makes her husband black, but on the other rejects it in a selective way so that her daughter's classification as multiracial may thereby be accommodated. We must understand that first-generation black/white multiracial identity involves the selective application of hypodescent together with a continuing veneration of white racial purity. Without these two phenomena, US first-generation black/white multiracial identity cannot exist.

This emphasis on first-generation black/white multiracial identity is a relatively recent occurrence in terms of its intensity. The first-generation distinction has had a life in the conversation surrounding multiracialism for years; however, until very recently it has been discussed primarily via informal venues. Its more formal appearance is a response to the general criticism that since all Afro-Americans have mixed ancestry, the notion of black/white multiracial identity is redundant and therefore irrelevant. One often encountered this criticism during the 1990s in the pages of Afro-American-oriented publications and from Afro-American political and cultural organizations opposed to the question of a federal multiracial category.

The key allegation is that since black/white multiracial identity is a distinction without a difference, the true goal of its adherents is to create a privileged and exclusionary identity separate from other Afro-Americans. Renee Romano reminds us of the impact of white mothers in this effort by noting that "the fact that some of those who most actively push for the legal recognition of multiracial status are the white parents of multiracial children only fuels suspicion that the real goal of the multiracialists is to distance their children from the stigma of being considered black."[9] The continuing success of the distinction without a difference criticism, for its logic is unimpeachable, has led some proidentity academics to champion the notion of first-generation black/white multiracial identity as a means of salvaging the privilege, exclusivity, and distinguishing cachet that multiracialism provides.

It will be useful, then, to turn to an in-depth assessment of the first-generation argument as put forth by academics writing in support of black/white multiracial identity. G. Reginald Daniel is probably the best of the current proidentity academics.[10] He has a sustained record of publication in the field of multiracial identity studies, and is one of the sub-discipline's pioneers. Daniel is also someone who has worked toward inscribing first-generation distinctiveness vis-à-vis the well-known mixed ancestry of Afro-Americans in general. As such, when we review Daniel's arguments on the question of first-generation black/white multiracial identity, we will find ourselves considering the best that has been offered to date.

Importantly, indeed first of all, Daniel shows himself to be a believer in biological race. He will likely never state that he is, but like so many other academics he also invokes the social race obfuscation in order to say one thing but actually do another. We see this clearly in Daniel's explanation that the first-generation identity is "derived from having one parent who is socially designated, and self-identified, as black, and one who is socially designated, and self-identified, as white, regardless of the multiple racial and cultural backgrounds in their parents' genealogy."[11] This is Daniel's variation on the now familiar formula for escorting biological race into the house through the backdoor of social race. As with all the others, it contains the same fatal logical inconsistency. If the child is to be considered first-generation multiracial because she or he is the biological child of these two socially designated parents, then it is biological race and not social designation that is the basis of the child's racial identity. As convenient as it might be, merely stating that the parents' multiple ancestral backgrounds are irrelevant hardly makes them so. One needs to actually provide something in the way of a compelling argument for that claimed irrelevance.

Daniel attempts to deflect this line of criticism as originating "in the misinterpretation of the discourse on multiracial identity as grounded in biological rather than ancestral notions of race," but his explanation is far from compelling.[12] According to Daniel, "biological notions of race and those based on ancestry may overlap, but they are not synonymous. The former is based on one's genetic inheritance irrespective of ancestral background. The latter is grounded in the backgrounds in one's lineage or genealogy, irrespective of genetic concerns, and is the basis of the new multiracial identity."[13] I fail to find any significant difference between these two propositions, however, as a person's ancestral background cannot be separated from her or his genetic inheritance. They do not merely overlap; they are two sides of the same coin.

My own backgrounds are sub-Saharan African and northern European. In what significant way does my sub-Saharan African background differ in terms of a genetic inheritance versus in terms of ancestry? In what significant way does my northern European background differ in terms of ancestry versus in terms of a genetic inheritance? How would it be possible to claim either my sub-Saharan African or northern European ancestries "irrespective of genetic concerns"? What sense would it make to talk about either my sub-Saharan African or northern European genetic inheritances irrespective of my ancestral background, irrespective of my lineage or genealogy? What Daniel is attempting here is to create the appearance of moving away from biological race, but his ancestral notion of race is precisely the same thing. And if it is not the same thing, then he is merely talking about ethnicity, which would contradict the elaborate formulations he has tried to set up in arguing for first-generation black/white multiracial identity qua a racial identity.

This tortured formulation is the basic argument for first-generation black/white multiracial identity. The need to veil the all-too-obvious link between biological race and multiracial identity leads to some interesting theoretical consequences. Notice in the following application of Daniel's formulation the twisted logic that results from the attempted masking of that relationship. Imagine two children, both with (for the sake of brevity only) unproblematically white mothers. Both fathers are Afro-American, and therefore have European and sub-Saharan African population mixture in their ancestries. Moreover, both fathers are biological brothers having the same set of parents. Both of these fathers are socially designated as black; however, the first father is self-identified as black while the second father is self-identified as multiracial. According to Daniel, the child of the first father is first-generation black/white multiracial but the child of the second father is not. This absurd consequence is a result of attempting to place a socially designated window-dressing on what is a biological function.

Nor is Daniel the only proidentity academic to fall victim to the logical inconsistency of the social race illusion. Marion Kilson also follows the familiar path of initially denying, then subsequently affirming, biological race. First, the denial: "Despite the intermingling of Native Americans, Europeans, Africans, and Asians in North America for nearly four centuries, Americans have found acknowledging this reality problematic within the framework of Northern European hegemony."[14] On reading Kilson's words we might be lulled into supposing that this is a good start, a critique of the US racial paradigm with an acknowledgment of the difficulties of overturning it. Yet, having made the obligatory denial, Kilson then signals her affirmation of biological race by approvingly citing Daniel's formulation on the very next page: "The carriers of this new blended identity are primarily . . . 'first generation' individuals."[15]

Kilson, like Daniel, also fumbles logically in attempting to put into action her own theory: "When I use the term 'Biracial American' to refer to people whose parents belong to different socially recognized racial groups, I appreciate that the racial heritage of many Americans is infinitely more complex."[16] Yet this claimed appreciation of complexity leads Kilson to the following astoundingly fallacious conclusion: "Among the Biracial young adults who participated in my research, several alluded to more complex racial heritages for their parents of color. At least one African American parent had a European American grandmother, while other African American parents claimed Native American as well as African American heritages. Nevertheless, since all project participants identified their birth parents as belonging to different racial groups, I consider all of them to be 'first generation' Biracial Americans."[17] As I have been arguing throughout this book, someone must call proidentity academics into account for this kind of nonsense masquerading as research. Kilson cannot simply create first-generation biracial Americans merely because it will be more convenient for her research if she does. We are long past the point at which this sort of flawed academic work can possibly be seen as acceptable. Such deliberate bending of data to reach foregone conclusions must be not only denounced clearly, but rejected firmly as well.

Kendra Wallace utilizes a slightly different organizational structure for conceptualizing racial mixture. In Wallace's formulation, "the term *mixed heritage* is used . . . to refer to recent (first, second, and third generation) multiple ethnic and racial heritage."[18] In Wallace's view, only the three most recent generations count in calculating a mixed heritage, and any mixture further back—even if it is more pronounced—is thereby erased. This kind of thinking results in the contradictory conclusion that an Afro-American with one white grandparent would be considered to be of mixed heritage, whereas an Afro-American with five white great-grandparents would not. As Jill Olumide muses, and I certainly agree with her, "the point at which 'mixed' ceases to be regarded as mixed is an interesting question."[19] For proidentity academics, it is clear that the point at which mixture is erased must be as near to the present as possible.

As I have indicated, Daniel is likely the best of the proidentity academics, and as such he has attempted to provide a somewhat more nuanced formulation of the first-generation argument than most of his counterparts. He has done this by positing three different kinds of black/white people. All three types are racially mixed, but they are each cast as being different from the others. We have already seen his definition of first-generation individuals as having parents both socially designated and self-identified as black and as white respectively. In addition to this first type, he posits "multigenerational" persons and "African Americans." The former "have parents, or even generations of ancestors, who have been viewed as black by society although their backgrounds include African American, European American, and other ancestries (particularly Native American); these individuals, and/or their parents and ancestors, have resisted identifying solely with the African American community."[20] Daniel's African Americans, on the other hand, "for the most part have multiple racial/cultural backgrounds but a single-racial/cultural identity as black."[21]

It is important to see what Daniel is doing here with this formulation. First of all, each of these three types of people is an Afro-American, of course; so the fracturing of Afro-American identity into three distinct types in this way is a rather strange stretch to say the least. One might be inclined to suppose that Daniel has mirrored my assessment earlier in this chapter of all Afro-Americans as being redundantly mixed-race, but he has not done that at all. What Daniel has done instead is to attempt to blur the distinction between biological race and social culture so as to make them interchangeable. Whereas I acknowledge that all Afro-Americans have European and sub-Saharan African population mixture in their ancestries, and that this makes them redundantly mixed-race, Daniel is saying something quite different. In the case of his multigenerationals he is talking about people who have identified as mixed-race as opposed to black, and in the case of African Americans he is talking about people who identify as black. This is a distinction based purely on personal choice, and as such it might change from year to year—presumably with significant impact for the assignation of first-generation multiracial identity to any relevant children under the parameters of Daniel's first-generation formulation.

Notice that in all three cases the persons in question have mixed ancestries, but the criterion of identity varies for each type—a sign that we have entered the realm of logical inconsistency. In the first case the criterion of identity is having socially designated and self-identified parents of different races, while in the second and third cases the criterion of identity is solely personal choice. For first-generation individuals Daniel leaves no choice—they are multiracial regardless, perhaps, of their own personal choice, as the exclusive criterion is how their parents are identified and how their parents identify themselves. For multigenerational persons the criterion is that they do not identify "solely with the African American community." Moreover, whereas culture is not a criterion of identity for multigenerationals, it is included as a criterion for African Americans. For the latter, the criterion is that they have a "single-racial/cultural identity as black." Thus it is somewhat difficult to evaluate these three identity options in comparison with each other.

I also find something of a false dilemma in the way in which multigenerationals merely need not identify "solely with the African American community," while African Americans have a "single-racial/cultural identity as black," as this arrangement seems to force people unnaturally into artificial groupings that may contradict the untidy and complicated lives they actually live. In other words, Daniel's identity options represent too simplistic a formula to capture accurately the complexity of the way people identify themselves, which is something of an ironic charge to be able to levy against a proponent of multiracial identity. As Tanya Hernández points out, "the community of biracial persons is not a monolith. There are a great number of biracial persons whose racial identity is rooted in blackness because of the political meaning of race in this society."[22] And to echo Hernández' important observation, such a political position in no way compels one to disavow one's multiple ancestries.

In Daniel's account, the "new multiracial identity . . . is displayed by individuals who attach equal value to their European American background and identify with European Americans without diminishing the value attached to their African American background and affinity with the experience of African Americans," but I question whether there is any real distinction to be made here.[23] Daniel presents no reason why a person could not value both backgrounds equally, identify with both backgrounds equally, and have equal affinity for both backgrounds but, because of the racist political realities of life in the United States, identify as black and not as multiracial. There is a great difference between identifying "with" and identifying "as." I can identify *with* you and *with* your situation without identifying *as* you. So there is no reason, in accordance with Daniel's own formulation, why an Afro-American could not identify *as* black and still identity *with* both backgrounds equally. Try as he might, Daniel simply is unable to define an exclusionary black/white multiracial identity in such a way as to preclude "regular" Afro-Americans from meeting it as well.

Kerry Ann Rockquemore is absolutely correct in her assertion that "the *idea* that multiracial people may have multiple ways in which they identify themselves is a complex reality that is incompatible and inconsistent with a singular push for separate status as multiracial."[24] In support of that singular push, however, and in order to force his first-generation theory to work, Daniel sets up a false, either/or scenario that is belied by everyday experience. Itabari Njeri makes this precise point when she writes that "we should never allow any *multiracial* person— either through ignorance or political calculation—to exoticize his identity at our expense. We should co-opt the position and assert that, as New World Blacks, we are multiethnic people; in doing so, we should make clear to ourselves and others that affirming our multiethnic ancestry and being 'Black' are not mutually exclusive."[25]

Itabari's concern is justified, for this is precisely where the erasure takes place in Daniel's formulation, as his African Americans in the third case are retrofitted and transformed into the monoracially black parents in the first case. It is critical to see the movement here; it is a movement from social race to biological race. Daniel's African Americans have "multiple racial/cultural backgrounds but a single-racial/cultural identity as black." So, what is key prior to the movement is that the criterion of racial identity appears to be personal choice, not biology. Thus biological race is at first avoided (seemingly) and the emphasis appears to be on the social. However, should one of Daniel's African Americans of "multiple racial/cultural backgrounds" procreate with a white partner, that African American becomes monoracially black. This is the occasion of the movement as well as the location of the erasure. The movement is from a social designation of race to a bio-logical designation, and the erasure is the disappearance of ancestral population mixture from the retrofitted black parent.

But, one might object, does Daniel not provide that this person is socially designated and self-identified as black, thereby leaving the matter in the realm of the social and not the biological? The answer to that objection is no, because the resulting child's first-generation multiracial status depends absolutely on the biological mating of these parents. Daniel's proviso that we may disregard the "multiple racial and cultural backgrounds in [the] parents' genealogy" is meaningless, for how can a first-generation black/white multiracial child come to be conceived absent the biological mating of two racially pure and racially distinct parents? This is the grand illusion of the first-generation position. Daniel's convenient caveat regarding the irrelevancy of the parents' actual ancestry is either a clumsy subterfuge or the kind of carelessness we have become accustomed to encountering in proidentity academic writing. Regardless, the caveat is meaningless.

Once we move from the social designation and self-identification of individuals to the birth of a child conceived by those two individuals, we have—if we are going to play the Raceland game—two choices in regard to the racial identity of that child: to base the child's racial identity on the same criterion as that of the parents (social, not biological), or to base the child's racial identity on a different criterion than that of the parents (biological, not social). The first choice is consistent and valid logically; the second choice is inconsistent and invalid logically. The first choice would require that, just as in the case of the parents, the child's racial identity must depend at least in part on the social designation imposed by outsiders, which would in many cases lead to the child being designated as black via hypodescent. This is why proidentity academics are forced into the second choice, to make the inconsistent move from social race for the parents to biological race for those parents' children.

What Daniel attempts to accomplish via that second choice is to provide the necessary social race window-dressing to seemingly move his formulation away from the foundation of biological race that undergirds it, but to then inject biological race at the critical point: the birth of a child conceived by two differently raced parents so that in some way—we are not told how—the biological mating of two supposedly socially raced parents results in the birth of a first-generation multiracial child. But if the child is first-generation multiracial precisely because she or he is the biological child of these two parents, then it absolutely must be biological race that is the operative mechanism, not the window-dressing of social race. This is an a priori logical necessity. If Daniel would allow that, should these same two parents adopt an Asian child, this Asian child would thereby become a first-generation black/white multiracial by virtue of the social designations and self-identifications of her or his parents, then a measure of logical consistency would be restored although the result would be an obvious absurdity. But if Daniel will not allow this outcome, then his formulation's trumpeting of social designation and self-identification is revealed to be completely spurious. He simply cannot have it both ways.

Several final examples bring to light additional logical flaws in Daniel's schema. Suppose a first-generation black/white multiracial boy grows up and becomes of age. Moreover, suppose that our young adult male becomes inspired politically to adopt a black self-definition and is also socially designated as black. Now, if this person should procreate with a white woman (an unproblematically racially pure one, for the sake of brevity of course) the resulting child—since the parent's black racial identity is a personal choice in Daniel's formulation—would be a first-generation black/white multiracial! In fact, our former first-generation black/white multiracial individual could sire an endless line of first-generation black/white multiracials as long as each was socially designated and self-identified as black by adulthood and then proceeded to procreate with whites.

Alternatively, a similar flaw makes itself known from the opposite direction. One wonders if a first-generation black/white multiracial child would lose her or his racial identity should the child's black father opt to subsequently change his former personal identity choice from black to something else, since a major criterion of first-generation identity—one of the child's parents being self-identified as black—would no longer apply. It does not matter whether or not one thinks such scenarios are in the least bit likely. What matters is that in a structural sense they expose huge logical flaws. In fact, "huge" does not convey my meaning adequately. These are logical flaws so outrageous and so absolutely fatal that they render the entire machination—first-generation, multigenerational, African American—dead in the water.

In attempting to craft a more nuanced theory so as to avoid the appearance of relying on biological race, Daniel has instead constructed a paradigm that has no internal logical consistency. One type of racial identity is based on a person's parents' social designation and self-identification, while the two other types of racial identity are based on how a person opts to identify—yet in all three cases the individuals concerned may in fact have precisely the same population mixtures in their respective ancestries. This fact and other absurdities are the result of trying to fabricate a theory that strives to do the impossible: make biological race disappear from view while still resulting in an outcome that is as eminently biologically racial as an eighteenth-century natural science treatise on race-mixing. In the end, Daniel's first-generation formulation is shown to be every bit as fallacious as those treatises were.

More is at stake here than merely pointing out the logical invalidity of the first-generation position, as noble a philosophical cause as that might be. As we shall see, despite its logical emptiness, the first-generation argument threatens to lead to the installation of a new, or at least altered, racial paradigm in the United States. As a prelude to considering that specific problem, I return to discussion of the historical erasure of Afro-Americans' mixed ancestry, for that erasure is central to constructing the altered paradigm. At base is the very simple goal that despite the centuries of population mixture that have taken place—not to mention the mixture that took place before the various parties arrived on the shores of British North America and the United States—Afro-American heterogeneity must be denied so that the meaningless distinction of black/white multiracial identity may be erected and maintained.

As Matthew Jacobson explains, "we might take note of and really examine the paradoxical reifying power of the 'multiracial' category for the notion of essentially fixed races that happen to 'mix' from time to time. The notion of a stable whiteness and a stable blackness that in some instances come together in multiracial hybridity seems to tip its hat to the complexity and the historical messiness of race; but it quietly effaces the long history of race mixing that is in fact the norm. . . . This history—a centuries-long history on all sides of the color lines—is utterly effaced by the 'multiracial' category, which posits 'mixture' as only an occasional phenomenon in a setting otherwise characterized by racial purity."[26]

To be sure, a measure of obeisance to past population mixture is usually granted by proidentity academics, but it is swept quickly aside as irrelevant in order that the case for first-generation multiraciality may be built. One of two tactics is typically employed in this endeavor. The first, considered above in the case of Daniel's theory, is to cloak biological race in the camouflage of social race and thereby institute what seems to be a new racial understanding. As we have seen, that attempt ultimately falls inward upon itself like the house of cards it is. The other tactic is to argue or otherwise imply that the past population mixture took place so long ago that it no longer matters. The idea, in other

words, is that Afro-Americans have in the intervening centuries reverted
back to simply being monoracially black in order that first-generation
black/white multiracial identity may have meaning.

The very serious problem with this tactic is that something of the
opposite effect has actually taken place instead. The further and further
we are removed from colonial and slave days, the more and more ances-
trally mixed the Afro-American population becomes. One might ask
how this can be, as it may at first seem somewhat counterintuitive. But
there is no contradiction, as the principle is a simple one. The Afro-
American population becomes ever more mixed even in the absence of
children conceived by ostensibly black and white parents, due to the
mechanism of internal miscegenation, which takes place every time two
Afro-Americans have a child together. The ancestral population mixture
in the histories of both mother and father are passed on to the child, so
that population-mixing involving sub-Saharan African and European
ancestries is happening even if no whites are party to a particular conception.

As Gunnar Myrdal pointed out correctly more than half a century
ago: "*Internal miscegenation* within the Negro group between individuals with varying degrees of white ancestry is, and will in the future be,
going on. The result is a tendency toward a slow but continuous equalization of Negro and white genes in the Negro people, decreasing the
relative numbers at both the black and white extremes and concentrating
the individuals ever closer to the average."[27] This is the "Browning of
America" that Joel Williamson has described and that is still happening
today despite any immigration from sub-Saharan Africa and the
Caribbean.[28] This is reality. The thirty million Afro-Americans in the
United States are already mixed. Any additional mixture—so-called
first-generation mixture—is irrelevant, is redundant, and adds nothing to
the ancestral richness already present.

Most Americans today suffer from a case of historical presentism
that causes them to inappropriately impose their own experiences onto
the world of the past. Thus they do not think to realize that the sub-
Saharan African slaves of 350 years ago do not look like the Afro-
Americans of today, except possibly in relatively isolated pockets such
as the Sea Islands. What Americans fail to see is that while a supposed
first-generation black/white person of today and his supposedly black
father of today may be indistinguishable from each other in terms of
which one is mixed and which one (supposedly) is not, the same would
surely not have been said in earlier times. The child of a sub-Saharan
African freeman and the lower-class white woman with whom he lived

in colonial Virginia would easily have been distinguishable visually, either from the child's sub-Saharan African father or from the child's European mother. The same would have been true of an Angolan slave and the child she conceived with her owner's son on a low-country plantation in South Carolina. These products of population mixture would have been readily distinguishable visually from either of their parents.

Williamson confirms this continuing trend in informing us that as part of the Browning of America, "'visibility' probably changed over the generations. A person whom the census taker in 1850 might have judged as a mulatto in 1920 might be judged as black. In brief, as the entire Negro population became lighter, both what was thought to be black and what was thought to be mulatto became lighter and mulattoes were counted as blacks in increasing numbers."[29] Most Americans today have not grasped this important historical fact, and instead they imagine that the so-called blacks of several hundred years ago looked like those of today. This is a useful illustration of why contrived formulations such as Daniel's first-generation schema are so profoundly doomed to failure, as all his supposedly different types—first-generation, multigenerational, African American—in general look like what most people would take to be Afro-Americans! One cannot tell which is which by merely looking at them. Because Afro-Americans have such significant amounts of population mixture in their personal histories, and because that population mixture continues to keep circulating via internal miscegenation, Afro-Americans cover the phenotypic gamut. This by itself gives lie to the notion that we can concoct in an artificial way some real category of people who are truly first-generation black/white multiracials. Logically, scientifically, historically—it just cannot be done. However, this cold fact hardly means that people nonetheless do not try.

Korgen illustrates such an attempt when she complains of many biracial individuals being "viewed and treated, by both black and white persons, as African Americans."[30] My incredulous response to this statement is to wonder in precisely what way they are not Afro-Americans. Indeed, they are every bit as Afro-Euro-American as any other Afro-American. That Korgen's complaint is registered in apparent genuine seriousness illustrates how far divorced from reality the proidentity position is. One need only delve just beneath the surface of black/white multiracial scholarship for these types of inanities to begin literally jumping off the page. When Korgen again manifests this phenomenon by describing one of her respondents as "someone who appears to be a light-skinned black person," we are left to ponder just what she really means.[31] In terms of skin color, Afro-Americans provide us an absolute-

ly unbroken continuum, from very lightest to very darkest. Korgen's
respondent is not "someone who appears to be a light-skinned black person"; rather he is a light-skinned Afro-American, with acknowledgment
of all the European ancestry that this designation ought quite rightly to
imply.

Of course, Korgen is interested very specifically in creating a false
distinction between black/white multiracials and Afro-Americans. As
such, her attempts to construct first-generation multiracials mark her as
one of the purveyors of white racial purity and as one of the erasers of
the Afro-American past's full measure of population mixture. This erasure happens continually, and generally without much protest, although
there is some here and there. Mark Christian points toward the superfi-
ciality of this erasure when he warns that "it would be facile to confine
the semantics surrounding multiracial peoples to that of a contemporary
phenomenon in suggesting that such persons are, for example, 'new
people.'"[32] In Christian's view, "the perspective suggesting that there is
a 'new' multiracial group *within* the African American community is
both myopic and ahistorical."[33] Njeri questions the possible motivations
of those who insist on replacing the Afro-American mixed historical
reality with a monoracial myth: "It is, perhaps, this chronic need to
stand in juxtaposition to the 'not-me' and point a denying finger that
compels many *multiracial* Americans, and their families, to demand that
their biological truth be acknowledged, and exoticized, while persistent-
ly and falsely referring to African Americans as *monoracial.*"[34]

Ann Morning looks to the practical effects of engaging in this myth:
"By obscuring the historic dimensions of American multiraciality—
emphasizing its newness but not its oldness—we may run the risk of
ignoring lessons that past racial stratification offers for understanding
today's outcomes."[35] Similarly, Eileen Walsh demonstrates additional
practical concerns over the potential falsification of present realities
should there be no challenge to this rewriting of the Afro-American
past; she warns that "losing sight of that historical vision, however, may
create a mirage of multiracialism—an illusion of integration and equality that provides an undeserved hubris about how far we have come and
blinds us to the difference between a masked multiracial heritage and an
acknowledged multiracial heritage."[36] Walsh makes a critical point here,
for the difference she refers to in fact actually shrouds fundamental
sameness. In other words, there is no useful difference between so-
called first-generation black/white multiracials and Afro-Americans, but
the false difference imposed by the multiracial myth hides that fact from
view and leads toward the threat of a new racial paradigm.

Multiracial activists and proidentity academics have been arguing since the 1990s that official recognition of multiracial identity will lead to the breakdown of the race concept in the United States. Their argument is that a multiracial category would blur and destabilize race-thinking in such a way that race itself would have to be abandoned as a means of inscribing difference. As Romano reports, some in the multiracial identity movement believe that "the rising numbers of multiracial children will undermine the whole concept of race as more and more people are born who do not fit into a single category," and that these children's "very existence . . . will undermine racial categories."[37] As with so many other assertions made under the multiracial banner, this prediction is always made with no support beyond the assertion itself. But would official recognition of multiracial identity be likely to have the ameliorative effect its adherents predict it would? There is no reason to think so, and there are several reasons for thinking it would not, the most important being the continued and unchallenged veneration of whiteness.

As Steven Ropp confesses somewhat wryly: "Persons of mixed, multiple, or ambiguous racial heritage are presumed to represent a challenge to racial thinking. After twenty-seven years of being one of these people, after eight years of doing research on various aspects of the mixed-race experience, and after four years of involvement with a specific social organization organized around 'multiracial' Asian American issues, I increasingly believe that the practice falls far short of the discourse."[38] Ropp's sardonic comment illustrates the gap between facile predictions of the impending destabilization of the US racial paradigm and the reality of the paradigm's utter stability.

First of all, it is important to understand that official recognition of multiracial identity would render it essentially the same as any other monoracial identity. It would simply be another nonwhite category within the paradigm. Once enshrined officially, and once having joined the other official racial designations, a multiracial category would be no different than those others it would have become associated with. Any destabilizing or deconstructive power the multiracial idea may have possessed in theory would be utterly lost if it became just another nonwhite racial category.[39] As we have seen, rather than deconstructing race, the notion of multiracial identity reinforces and is reinforced by the same biological constructions that underlie the US racial paradigm. All the same, the success of multiracial ideology in the popular realm—a success now bolstered by proidentity academics—has led to blind acceptance of the notion of mixed-race identity and of a growing army of racially ambiguous teenagers as a destabilizing threat to the US racial paradigm. But how much of a challenge is black/white multiraciality really, if all that is meant is that some teens may now be able to distance themselves from blackness while those who are less ambiguous visually cannot?

In general, what we find is that racially ambiguous persons are not destabilizing race at all. In addition to falling victim to the presentism that clouds the historical reality of what racially mixed people may or may not look like, most commentators make the mistake of viewing this alleged racial deconstruction only through the darker end of the continuum. By doing so, they fail to see that the other end of the continuum—the white end—remains as fixed, stable, and pure as always. In other words, when people assert that some particular black/white person is ambiguous racially, they typically mean that the person is not confidently categorizable as black. Rarely do they mean that the person is not confidently categorizable as white. To be sure, the doors to whiteness may be breached occasionally, but in the main they stand as closely guarded as ever.

What we are therefore witnessing is not the destabilization of race, per se, but rather the fracturing of blackness without an attendant fracturing of whiteness. The erasure of historical Afro-American heterogeneity via the first-generation scheme and also more generally, leads to the ahistorical retrofitting of Afro-Americans as monoracially black. What this means is that Afro-Americans may be fracturing into at least two groups: black nonwhites and seeming nonblack nonwhites, with so-called racially ambiguous black/white multiracials beginning to move toward that seeming nonblack nonwhite status. Of course, the critical point is that the latter are still nonwhites, albeit with a higher status in the racial hierarchy than "regular" Afro-Americans. But this is not a fracturing of the entire race concept itself, for, as I have indicated, whiteness still remains mythically pure and at the top of the hierarchy. One thousand instances of wondering if the racially ambiguous person is black fail to equal even one instance of wondering if the racially ambiguous person is white. Most people do not even realize that what they think is the deconstruction of race is really and merely the fracturing of blackness, along with the reinscription of monoracial blackness for those who are unambiguous either physically or ideologically, and a coextensive reaffirmation of white racial purity. As such, this is a conceptual block that complements the hegemony of the US racial paradigm in perfect fashion.

This is a function, it seems to me, of a little-considered aspect of hypodescent. While most people see hypodescent as meaning that any known or detectable sub-Saharan African ancestry renders an individual black, there is a corollary meaning as well: that any known or detectable sub-Saharan African ancestry also ensures that an individual is non-white. It is this latter sense that is operative in the case of multiracial identity and its failure to destabilize race. Persons who see themselves as first-generation black/white multiracials are not breaking down any aspects of the US racial paradigm. They may have lighter skin, they may have features marking them as ambiguously black or as just ambiguous in general, and they may be able to claim with success that they are not black, but they are in no sense accepted as white as long as their sub-Saharan African ancestry is known.

Jane Lazarre pointedly and correctly challenges biraciality's supposed deconstructive power in writing about her sons Adam and Khary. Lazarre considers biraciality to be a problematic concept, "as if young men with brown skins can ever be considered 'part white' in America; as if Adam, now an actor, can audition for 'white' parts in film, TV, or most theater; as if Khary, a young Black man walking on the streets late at night, can expect to be treated by the police like a young white man because his mother is white."[40] And this is the critical point, for minor alterations to the US racial paradigm are insignificant to the paradigm's continuing power as long as the pure and hierarchical status of whiteness remains unchallenged and unchanged. The paradigm will happily accommodate nonblack nonwhites as happily as it accommodates black nonwhites, since in either case whiteness remains undefiled and at the top of the hierarchy. If we may be sure of anything in regard to race in the United States, it is that the borders of whiteness are as heavily fortified and as fiercely defended today as they have ever been.

An increased distance from traditional conceptions of blackness is currently not being met with an equivalent increased nearness to traditional conceptions of whiteness. Thus, from popular entertainers and sports figures to the ubiquitous ambiguous females who populate so many television commercials and glossy magazine advertisements, some black/white persons may move away from blackness in some degree or other, but they do not really move toward whiteness. Caroline Streeter makes this plain in her comment that "this kind of multicultural imagery makes racially mixed people symbolic embodiments of antidiscrimination while using their images to mask persistent race-based inequalities."[41] I want to take a moment to clarify my meaning here, for it may seem counterintuitive. What I mean is this: as long as black/white multiracials cannot become white providing their sub-Saharan African ancestry is known (and they most certainly cannot), there really is no sense in which they truly approach whiteness in any degree. They may distance themselves from blackness, and they may move upward within the hierarchy of the US racial paradigm, but actually approaching whiteness itself is a Sisyphean enterprise. As has been the case for centuries, people of sub-Saharan African descent are accepted as white only by traveling the road of racial passing.

The notion of first-generation black/white multiraciality facilitates this fracturing of Afro-American historicity on one the hand just as it facilitates the continuing solidification of the mythical purity of whiteness on the other. Not only does the first-generation machination serve in a counterfeit deconstructive role, but it also works toward a more practical result. The practical result to which I am referring is the shifting of the US racial paradigm to accommodate the additional nonwhite category of "multiracial." As I have argued, neither first-generation black/white multiraciality nor a more official recognition of multiracial identity will lead to any deconstructing of the US racial paradigm; however, they could very well bring about an important alteration to that paradigm.

Charles Gallagher warns of the dangerous development of a new, black/nonblack paradigm. He is concerned "that we are currently experiencing a 'racial redistricting' where the borders of whiteness are expanding to include those groups who until quite recently would have been outside the boundaries of the dominant group."[42] In Gallagher's view, "as whites and other nonblack groups inhabit a common racial ground the stigma once associated with interracial relationships between these groups is diminishing."[43] As indicated above, I do not agree with the notion of a strict, black/nonblack paradigm, because in my view the status of whiteness will not allow it; however, I do share Gallagher's concern insomuch as other groups may be gravitating upward toward the loftier end of the hierarchy while Afro-Americans remain stuck at the bottom. This is the operationalization of what Lewis Gordon refers to when he states that "blackness, in the end, functions as a constant, underlying mark of racialization as does no other racial designation. Its persistence suggests that the fluidity of racial identities points upward in continuing spirals of potential whiteness."[44] Let there be no doubt that the first-generation project represents precisely just such an attempted movement.

Walsh as well sees the danger of this development. Commenting on the multiracial identity movement, she states that although "the movement's contributions are laudable, an unintended consequence of the multiracial project to bend the color line in this country may be the further disenfranchisement of those people of color who do not fit the newly evolving 'multiracial' racial category."[45] In this she echoes Herbert Gans, who cautions that "today's multiracial hierarchy could be replaced by what I think of as a dual or bimodal one consisting of 'nonblack' and 'black' population categories, with a third 'residual' category for the groups that do not, or do not yet, fit into the basic dualism. . . . The hierarchy is new only insofar as the old white-nonwhite dichotomy may be replaced by a nonblack-black one, but it is hardly new for blacks, who are likely to remain at the bottom once again."[46]

Nor is this concern merely about the passive effects of first-generation black/white multiracial identity in engendering an altered paradigm. It is also about the motivations of the collective multiracial identity movement as a whole, including its academic support wing. Stephen Small gestures toward the movement's questionable social compass in pointing out that "much of the focus of the movement is on the psychological issues involved in identity formation, and is frequently indifferent to the social consequences of the demands."[47] Kim Williams wonders about those motivations as she asks, "are Multiracial Movement activists well positioned to, and seriously concerned about waging an assault against institutional and other forms of racism, or is this movement simply another interest group marketing a fashionable identity at the expense of established minority populations?"[48]

Similarly, Heather Dalmage questions the stimulus behind the political connections that have been made by movement organizations in recent years. Her analysis is that "multiracial organizations have continued to link arms with conservative organizations such as Ward Connerly's American Civil Rights Institute, an organization dedicated to dismantling group-based protections. For instance, at the 'Multiracial Leadership Round Table 2000 Census: A Discussion About Our Choices,' Connerly was inducted into the 2000 Racial Harmony Hall of Fame. The award was created by the conservative multiracial organization, A Place For Us Ministry for Interracial Couples."[49] We may recall as well former Speaker of the House Newt Gingrich's positively oily co-optation of the multiracial identity movement, particularly in connection with Project RACE.[50] Leaving no possible room for misinterpretation, Mary Texeira is even more forthright in stating that "this movement is really about who is white(r) and who is not white."[51]

Apprising us of the need for vigilance, Hernández stresses that "the simultaneous growth of multiracial discourse and civil rights retrenchment should alert the MCM [Multiracial Category Movement] to the appropriation of its identity movement by others more concerned with dismantling social-justice programs."[52] Whether the co-optation was welcomed or not, the multiracial identity movement has been co-opted by various far-right factions over the years, sometimes with, as noted above, the full support of movement constituents.

In any case, there is a sense that the activist element has possibly faded from the political scene as much as it has faded from the debate scene (see the introduction to this book). As the 2010 census approaches, there has not been the kind of open agitation for a separate multiracial category that there was at the same point prior to the 2000 census. It may be that multiracial identity activists are satisfied enough at present with the "check all that apply" approach, that they have chosen to not advocate a separate category for 2010. It may also be that such activism is either yet to come or is already happening behind the scenes. In any case, the current landscape would seem to justify Reynolds Farley's assertion that the "social movement that led to the change in racial identification has not been active in the years since census data were collected. It has faded."[53]

It must be stated, however, that even should it be that the political wing of the multiracial identity movement has fallen into inactivity, this would not prevent the movement itself from being co-opted still further by far-right interests. Nor would it prevent the continuation of the everyday, popular entrenchment of the first-generation thesis and black/white multiracial identity in general. This happens regardless of the presence or absence of political maneuvering by multiracial identity activist leaders or their organizations. It is aided as well by the work of proidentity academics such as Brown, Daniel, Kilson, and Korgen, whose internally inconsistent writings are nonetheless given the stamp of scholarly authenticity by virtue of the fact that those writings have heretofore not received the critical challenge necessary to call them into question. As bad as the current and fallacious US racial paradigm is (and let there be no doubt that I consider it a horrible thing), the alterations discussed above—whether the fully bimodal model suggested by Gallagher and Gans or a model in which Asians, Native Americans, and multiracials all ascend toward the top of the hierarchy while Afro-Americans are left remaining at the bottom of the scale—are dangerous potentialities we should be on continuous guard against.

This is the insidiousness of the argument for first-generation black/white multiracial identity. As we have seen, the erasure of the mixed Afro-American historical reality and the corresponding erecting of the first-generation mirage work hand-in-hand to keep those Afro-

Americans who are not ambiguous enough by today's standards mired at the bottom of the racial hierarchy. As Romano explains, "this kind of thinking might contribute to the emergence of a privileged mixed-race class between blacks and whites."[54] At the very least, as Hernández makes clear, "in such a racial caste system, it is impossible to acknowledge mixed race persons officially without actually elevating the status of those who can claim to be other than 'pure' Black, no matter how egalitarian the intent of the MCM."[55]

In Hernández' view, the deleterious effects of white privilege combined with the motivations of some of those supporting black/white multiracial identity complicate "the MCM assertion that the unique life experiences of mixed-race persons alone justify a separate racial classification. For instance, one White mother of mixed-race children has related the desire to impart to her son the privilege of walking about the world without being concerned that others will find him racially threatening and thereby presume him criminal."[56] Clearly, the physical appearance of this woman's son will not change, so it is precisely and only through the altering of the paradigm and the movement of such alleged first-generation multiracials upward within the paradigm that her son's status can possibly change in the way this mother hopes.

Writing in response to Hernández' arguments, Reginald Robinson asks, "what if white mothers wish in reality to confer a social largess on biracial or multiracial children? This effort too bespeaks of irony. How do we as a society confer a property interest on a biracial or multiracial person's whiteness without simultaneously benefiting her blackness?"[57] Robinson's presumed benefit to one's blackness does not obtain because the reality is that the racial enterprise is a zero-sum game. The multiracial person's blackness is not benefited at all in this case; rather, it is merely to some degree more tolerated. But even were we to imagine that some benefiting of blackness did actually occur, any such benefiting would be to the sole advantage of the particular biracial person in question only. Is Robinson arguing that we should support a system wherein the blackness of biracial people is benefited by its association with whiteness, while the blackness of "regular" Afro-Americans is not? Again, the false distinction of the first-generation position further disadvantages those not privileged with being perceived as possessing a portion of whiteness. Or is Robinson merely intending something similar to what Paul Rosenblatt, Terri Karis, and Richard Powell have in mind when they inform us of the happy news that "a biracial child can gain from educational benefits available to children of color"?[58]

Rather than taking a firm stand against the racist US racial paradigm under which all nonwhites labor, the first-generation position seeks instead to allow those so designated to claim a portion of whiteness (even though they cannot actually become white as long as their sub-Saharan African ancestry is known), and to thereby facilitate their movement upward within the paradigm to the disadvantage of others whose station at the bottom remains fixed. Daniel states as much in his explanation of the multiracialist motivation: "Generated by racist pressure that has rewarded whiteness and punished blackness, the tactics of resistance devised by multiracial individuals have been less a reaction to the forced denial of their European American ancestry than to the subordination and the denial of privileges that such ancestry is supposed to guarantee."[59] Although I am singularly unimpressed by Daniel's excuse, I do appreciate its honesty.

Notes

1. Joel Williamson, *New People: Miscegenation and Mulattoes in the United States* (New York: Free Press, 1980), 125.

2. Danzy Senna, "The Mulatto Millennium," in *Half and Half: Writers on Growing Up Biracial and Bicultural,* ed. Claudine C. O'Hearn (New York: Pantheon, 1998), 22.

3. Jill Olumide's observation that "the white category, it might be argued, is hybridity successfully passing for white," is instructive. Jill Olumide, *Raiding the Gene Pool: The Social Construction of Mixed Race* (London: Pluto, 2002), 153.

4. Indeed, part of this point is made for the sake of argument only, as any racial unmixedness of modern sub-Saharan Africans, or possibly Caribbean peoples, is an open question as well.

5. Jayne O. Ifekwunigwe, "Introduction: Rethinking 'Mixed Race' Studies," in *"Mixed Race" Studies: A Reader,* ed. Jayne O. Ifekwunigwe (London: Routledge, 2004), 3.

6. I cited several examples of this in Chapter 1.

7. Kathleen Korgen, *From Black to Biracial: Transforming Racial Identity Among Americans* (Westport: Praeger, 1999).

8. US House Subcommittee on Census, Statistics, and Postal Personnel, Committee on Post Office and Civil Service, *Hearings on the Review of Federal Measurements of Race and Ethnicity,* 103rd Cong., 1st sess., April 14, June 30, July 29, November 3, 1993, testimony by Susan R. Graham, June 30, 1993, 120.

9. Renee Romano, *Race Mixing: Black-White Marriage in Postwar America* (Cambridge: Harvard University Press, 2003), 284.

10. To those who might feel that I am slighting Naomi Zack here, I respond that I do not consider her to be strictly proidentity, although she leans in that direction on occasion.

11. G. Reginald Daniel, *More Than Black? Multiracial Identity and the New Racial Order* (Philadelphia: Temple University Press, 2002), 102.

12. Ibid., 178.

13. Ibid.

14. Marion Kilson, *Claiming Place: Biracial Young Adults of the Post–Civil Rights Era* (Westport: Bergin and Garvey, 2001), 3.

15. Quoted in Kilson, *Claiming Place,* 4.

16. Kilson, *Claiming Place,* 6.

17. Ibid.

18. Kendra Wallace, *Relative/Outsider: The Art and Politics of Identity Among Mixed Heritage Students* (Westport: Ablex, 2001), x.

19. Olumide, *Raiding the Gene Pool,* 153.

20. Daniel, *More Than Black?* 6.

21. Ibid., 106.

22. Tanya K. Hernández, "'Multiracial' Discourse: Racial Classifications in an Era of Color-Blind Jurisprudence," *Maryland Law Review* 57, no. 97 (1998): 113.

23. G. Reginald Daniel, "Multiracial Identity in Global Perspective: The United States, Brazil, and South Africa," in *New Faces in a Changing America: Multiracial Identity in the 21st Century,* eds. Loretta Winters and Herman DeBose (Thousand Oaks, CA: Sage, 2003), 280.

24. Kerry Ann Rockquemore, "Deconstructing Tiger Woods: The Promise and the Pitfalls of Multiracial Identity," in *The Politics of Multiracialism: Challenging Racial Thinking,* ed. Heather M. Dalmage (Albany: State University of New York Press, 2004), 134.

25. Itabari Njeri, "The Last Plantation," in *"Mixed Race" Studies,* ed. Ifekwunigwe, 300.

26. Matthew F. Jacobson, "History, Historicity, and the Census Count by Race," in *The New Race Question: How the Census Counts Multiracial Individuals,* eds. Joel Perlmann and Mary C. Waters (New York: Russell Sage Foundation, 2002), 260.

27. Gunnar Myrdal, *An American Dilemma: The Negro Problem and Modern Democracy* (New York: Harper and Brothers, 1944), 135.

28. Williamson, *New People,* chap. 3.

29. Ibid., 114.

30. Korgen, *From Black to Biracial,* 62.

31. Ibid., 63.

32. Mark Christian, *Multiracial Identity: An International Perspective* (New York: St. Martin's, 2000), 106.

33. Ibid., 115.

34. Njeri, "The Last Plantation," 298.

35. Ann Morning, "New Faces, Old Faces: Counting the Multiracial Population Past and Present," in *New Faces in a Changing America,* eds. Winters and DeBose, 41.

36. Eileen T. Walsh, "Ideology of the Multiracial Movement: Dismantling the Color Line and Disguising White Supremacy?" in *The Politics of Multiracialism,* ed. Dalmage, 223.

37. Romano, *Race Mixing,* 283, 288.

38. Steven Ropp, "Do Multiracial Subjects Really Challenge Race? Mixed Race Asians in the United States and the Caribbean," in *"Mixed Race" Studies,* ed. Ifekwunigwe, 264.

39. I provide a fuller explication of this particular thesis in Rainier Spencer, "Beyond Pathology and Cheerleading: Insurgency, Dissolution, and Complicity in the Multiracial Idea," in *The Politics of Multiracialism,* ed. Dalmage, 116–119.

40. Jane Lazarre, *Beyond the Whiteness of Whiteness: Memoir of a White Mother of Black Sons* (Durham, NC: Duke University Press, 1996), xvii.

41. Caroline A. Streeter, "The Hazards of Visibility: 'Biracial' Women, Media Images, and Narratives of Identity," in *New Faces in a Changing America,* eds. Winters and DeBose, 311.

42. Charles A. Gallagher, "Racial Redistricting: Expanding the Boundaries of Whiteness," in *The Politics of Multiracialism,* ed. Dalmage, 60.

43. Ibid.

44. Lewis R. Gordon, "Race, Biraciality, and Mixed Race," in *"Mixed Race" Studies,* ed. Ifekwunigwe, 159.

45. Walsh, "Ideology of the Multiracial Movement," 231.

46. Herbert Gans, "The Possibility of a New Racial Hierarchy in the Twenty-First-Century United States," in *The Cultural Territories of Race: Black and White Boundaries,* ed. Michele Lamont (Chicago: University of Chicago Press, 1999), 371.

47. Stephen Small, "Colour, Culture, and Class: Interrogating Interracial Marriage and People of Mixed Racial Descent in the USA," in *Rethinking "Mixed Race,"* eds. David Parker and Miri Song (London: Pluto, 2001), 126.

48. Kim Williams, "Linking the Civil Rights and Multiracial Movements," in *The Politics of Multiracialism,* ed. Dalmage, 90.

49. Heather M. Dalmage, introduction to *The Politics of Multiracialism,* ed. Dalmage, 4.

50. Rainier Spencer, "Census 2000: Assessments in Significance," in *New Faces in a Changing America,* eds. Winters and DeBose, 105–108. I discuss both Gingrich and Connerly in these pages.

51. Mary Thierry Texeira, "The New Multiracialism: An Affirmation of or an End to Race As We Know It?" in *New Faces in a Changing America,* eds. Winters and DeBose, 33.

52. Hernández, "'Multiracial' Discourse," 138.

53. Reynolds Farley, "Racial Identities in 2000: The Response to the Multiple-Race Response Option," in *The New Race Question,* eds. Perlmann and Waters, 58.

54. Romano, *Race Mixing,* 283.

55. Hernández, "'Multiracial' Discourse," 208.

56. Ibid., 119–120.

57. Reginald L. Robinson, "The Shifting Race-Consciousness Matrix and the Multiracial Category Movement: A Critical Reply to Professor Hernández," *Boston College Third World Law Journal* 20, no. 2 (Spring 2000): 276.

58. Paul C. Rosenblatt, Terri A. Karis, and Richard Powell, *Multiracial Couples: Black & White Voices* (Thousand Oaks, CA: Sage, 1995), 196.

59. Daniel, *More Than Black?* 82–83.

5

The Road Forward

Ray Stantz: "Hey; where d'these stairs go?"
Peter Venkman: "They go up."
                                    —From the film *Ghostbusters*[1]

W here does the field of multiracial identity studies go from here? This is an important question because, as the field is still relatively new, its shape is not yet fully determinate. When I say that the field is relatively new, I am of course aware of important work done on the subject of multiracial identity long before the current flourishing of scholarly publishing that began in the early 1990s. One can certainly look back to Joel Willamson's *New People* (1980), to John Mencke's *Mulattoes and Race Mixture* (1979), or indeed to Edward Reuter's *The Mulatto in the United States* (1918) for examples of earlier, single-authored, scholarly monographs on multiracial identity studies.[2] As significant as these earlier works were, though, they were occasional, independent volumes rather than riposting participants in an ongoing scholarly dialectic on the subject.

However, we are now approaching rapidly—if indeed we have not already reached—a critical mass of current scholarship that holds the promise of pushing the field forward to ever higher planes of critical, intellectual inquiry. Metatheorists of multiracial identity studies, because they are not burdened by belief in biological race or by the inherent bias of engaging in emotion-laden cheerleading, are showing the way in forging the path ahead. One question this book has considered is whether the proidentity branch of multiracial identity studies is a fellow traveler with the metatheoretical branch on that road forward. My conclusion is that, at present, it clearly is not.

The four major scholarly works of pro–multiracial identity that I have examined in this book each fail in significant ways to measure up to the challenge of advancing the proidentity position much beyond the intellectual level evidenced by the nonscholar activists of the 1990s.[3] I chose to examine these four texts because they represent the best the proidentity perspective has to date put together and published in the single-authored, monograph format. I chose them because they are recent, single-authored, scholarly texts that promised to deliver comprehensive and cutting-edge work in a field of study that has been witness to far too much of an "anything goes" attitude in its brief existence.

Unfortunately, the reality is that these texts, as well as the other supporting proidentity work I have cited, provide essentially more of the same. This is not to say that everything in those four books is wrong, or that there is nothing of value that each of them might tell us. But it is to say, and I do so with absolutely no equivocation, that each of the three interview studies is as a whole inadequate; and that the single theoretical text is inadequate at least as regards one of its central arguments—namely its justification of first-generation black/white multiracial identity.

The three interview studies, authored by Ursula Brown, Marion Kilson, and Kathleen Korgen, are each flawed in a fatal way by severely unrepresentative research subject pools providing data that are then generalized illegitimately to broader populations. Even though Brown is less overt in this regard than are Kilson and Korgen, the normative advice she gives based on her unrepresentative data as well as the numerous instances of psychobabble in her text serve to invalidate her study. In general, all three texts suffer from being insubstantial, error-filled entries in a field of study whose two primary branches (metatheory on the one hand and proidentity advocacy on the other) are clearly moving in two opposing directions—one up, the other down. Factual inaccuracy, carelessness, and the cheerleading bias generated by the crusader perspective from which they are written, all function to limit further whatever scholarly merit these texts might lay claim to.

In Daniel's case, given that the first-generation thesis appears to be the trajectory along which proidentity academics are aligning themselves currently, and given his prominent status within the field, the failure of his first-generation thesis is significant. As I have noted several times, Daniel is likely the very best of those academics whom I consider to be avowedly proidentity. He is looked to for guidance and for scholarly support by academic writers who share that proidentity ideology, who cite him approvingly, and who utilize his work in structuring their own contributions. In my view, he is at present the clear leader of the proidentity branch of the field of multiracial identity studies, and also the chief academic reference source for nonscholar activists. As such, his insupportable notion of first-generation black/white multiracial identity—in particular its disquieting philosophical porousness—deals a major blow to the intellectual validity of the ideological position favoring official acceptance of black/white multiracial identity.

Much will doubtless be made of the connection I have drawn between the flaws of the three interview studies and their authorship by white women academics who happen to have maternal and other close family relations to black/white persons. As I mentioned in Chapter 1, I am in no sense suggesting that white women should not write academic books on the subject of black/white multiracial identity. What I am instead pointing out is that being a white mother or close relative of a black/white child is no guarantee *in and of itself* that an author has anything of value to contribute to the field of multiracial identity studies. More than merely this is required for an author to make the case that she or he possesses the scholarly credentials and propounds factually correct and logically consistent arguments of the type that recommend themselves to serious engagement with the discourse of the field.

More is required, as well, than merely being a self-identified black/white person, of whatever supposed generation. What is required is academic objectivity, freedom from emotional bias, a willingness to conduct real research, and the care and attention to detail that marks the scholarly endeavor as the time-honored vocation it is. What is required is genuine respect for the field of multiracial identity studies, and the willingness to undertake at least the same kind of minimal literature review one would expect of one's own graduate students.

Do I, in levying these criticisms, envision myself as the sole gatekeeper of what is high-quality work and what is not in the field of multiracial identity studies? No, I most certainly do not. Rather, I see it as the scholarly obligation of each of us who writes in this subdiscipline to offer our very best, most careful work, and to challenge and refute work that fails to meet minimum scholarly muster. I have endeavored to do precisely that in this book, and I would hope that scholars who disagree with my arguments will subject what I have written here to the same kind of rigorous, demanding, logical analysis.

High-quality intellectual back-and-forth is what will lead to the kind of fertile dialectic that can truly advance the field by causing each of us who participate in it to ensure that our research efforts, our theories, our logical argumentation, and our academic prose are the very best they can be before we publish. Resisting the entry of sloppy, careless, academically frivolous work (whether proidentity or metatheoretical) into the discourse makes us all better by allowing us to concentrate our efforts on dealing with serious arguments in the service of solving serious problems. In short, we all should be referees rather than cheerleaders.

Am I attempting here a sort of "end run" to silence the proidentity position permanently by arguing that, in itself, it has no place in the discourse? No, that is not at all my intent. What I am saying is that academics who favor the proidentity position need to do a far better job of representing it than they have done to date. I have argued that the concept of multiracial identity is inextricably bound up with the idea of biological race, and as such is as fallacious as the US racial paradigm that undergirds it. To the extent that proidentity academics have attempted to disguise the necessary bond between their project and biological race, we have seen the fatally absurd logical inconsistencies that are the inevitable result. In my view, as long as the project is to construct a multiracial identity, with or without the fiction of biological race—but especially by attempting to evade that necessary association—it will be doomed to failure. However, I invite proponents of the proidentity view to prove me wrong through the use of persuasive, nonemotional arguments that are consistent philosophically and valid logically.

Academic advocates of multiracial identity might begin to right their philosophical ship by admitting openly that they believe in and endorse the concept of biological race. While this would, for obvious reasons, be hugely problematic, it would at least be more honest intellectually than continuing to maintain the transparent pretense that they do not. If there is anything to which the metaphor of the emperor having no clothes on applies, it is to this unconvincing charade.[4]

They must also begin to cease supporting every misplaced idea of the nonscholar activists, and to especially reject strongly those that are the most ludicrous. We may consider briefly the multiracial medical fallacy as a case in point of academics who, although they should know better, nonetheless follow the lead of nonscholar activists who often really have no idea what they are talking about. On July 20, 1996, I attended the "Multiracial Solidarity March on Washington," at which Ruth White, cofounder of A Place For Us Ministry for Interracial Couples (see Chapter 4), concluded her address with the assertion that "Rod Carew's daughter might be alive today . . . if the fact that . . . if they would have had a multiracial category for her, and had let her identify all of who she is."[5] White was referring to the untimely death of former professional baseball player Rod Carew's daughter Michelle from leukemia in the spring of 1996, and using that unfortunate death as justification for a federal multiracial category. Despite the emotional tug at one's heartstrings, this perpetuation of the multiracial medical myth by others only managed to make the Carews' misfortune sadder than it already was.

At any moment there are a fixed number of donors registered with the National Marrow Donor Program (NMDP). Regardless of the various racial categorizations that might be applied to these donors, there are only so many of them. The problem is numbers and diversity, not the lack of a particular category with which to self-identify. According to the NMDP's own literature: "The Program could accomplish even more if its Registry of volunteer donors was larger and more diverse. A majority of the volunteer donors in the NMDP Registry are Caucasian. While the NMDP welcomes everyone who is willing to volunteer, there is a critical need for more minority donors to help the many minority patients searching the Registry. By diversifying the Registry, the NMDP will be able to offer all patients a chance of finding an unrelated marrow donor."[6]

The key is diversity. Having as many different people join the NMDP registry as possible—regardless of whether they identify personally as Afro-American, Asian, or multiracial—is the answer to marrow transplant needs. The unfounded claim that establishing a federal multiracial category will lead to more patient-donor matches is cruel in its simplemindedness. Adding a federal multiracial classification will neither enroll more donors in the NMDP nor make the current donors suddenly viable for any particular patient. The only thing that can lead to more patient-donor matches is an increase in the number and diversity of donors, no matter how they might identify themselves racially. The same basic point may be made about the medical issue in general. Medical diagnoses must be made and medical treatments must be given based on individual conditions and individual family histories, not on the specious notion that some grouping of completely dissimilar people under a unitary multiracial heading will provide anything approaching medically relevant information.[7]

The nonscholar activist ranks are a continual source of precisely this type of factual inaccuracy, which should be corrected at every possible opportunity by academics who ought to display the benefits of more refined critical-thinking skills. Yet witness the position that Korgen takes on this issue vis-à-vis the multiracial advocacy organization Project RACE, whose executive director, nonscholar activist Susan Graham, was highlighted in the book's introduction and Chapters 3 and 4. In a discussion in which she writes approvingly of Project RACE's medical rationale for a federal multiracial category, Korgen reports that "the implications of such a category extend well beyond the political realm," and that the "lack of consideration of multiracial persons in reference to prescriptive drug use is one issue of particular concern" to Project RACE.[8] Korgen then relates the example of a pharmaceutical company's new hypertension drug to make this point: "They recommended that white persons take one milligram and black persons consume two milligrams per dosage. When questioned what size dosage multiracial persons should consume, the company admitted they had no idea. No multiracial persons were included in the clinical trials of the drug, emphasizing the fact that recognition of such a category is important not only for the psychological and social well-being of this population, but also for their physical health."[9]

Of course Korgen has missed completely the greater point in her own example. It seems not to have occurred to Korgen that for a pharmaceutical company to suggest *any* particular dosages based purely on patients' own self-identified racial categorizations is itself tantamount to medical malpractice. What sense would it make for a black-identifying person to take two milligrams of this drug if this person has a white mother but is unaware of it because she was adopted? What sense would it make for another black-identifying person to take two milligrams of this drug if he has a white grandparent on each side of his family but identifies so strongly as black that even were a federal multiracial category available it would hold no interest for him? Yet these are two persons who would consider themselves black, and who would be prescribed and who would presumably take the two-milligram dosage just as would a black-identifying person who was aware of no white ancestry in her heritage. As in a previous case (see Chapter 3), Korgen here again makes precisely the opposite point than she intends. Rather than providing any evidence of a medical justification for a federal multiracial category, Korgen's example makes painfully clear the very real dangers of imprudently—indeed, outrageously—prescribing medicines based on the fallacy of biological race.

What is evident is that there is no appreciable difference between nonscholar activists White and Graham and proidentity scholar Korgen on the fallacious issue of multiracial medical concerns being alleviated by a federal multiracial category. As long as scholarly cheerleaders are willing to give their stamp of academic approval to the more outlandish and factually vacant nonsense propagated by nonscholar activists, the proidentity branch will remain vulnerable to charges of carelessness and sloppiness.

There is no doubt that many Americans believe in the myth of biological race and in a multiracial fantasy derived from that belief. Clearly, some of these people have invested tremendous amounts of psychological and emotional capital in constructing for themselves personal identities that revolve around their assignment to a biological multiracial group. Precisely because they believe in biological race, these individuals are frustrated, insulted, and even outraged when others do not cooperate in assigning to them the biological multiracial categorization they have assigned to themselves. That their frustration and anger are developed in the service of accommodating themselves to a false consciousness is of little consequence, as they are engaged so deeply with the false consciousness that facts, science, and logic are unable to make any impression.

This is the landscape encountered by those who choose to enter the academic field of multiracial identity studies. There are at least two basic paths one can take in response to alighting upon this landscape. One path is to agree with the false consciousness of biological race and with the myth of multiracial identity it makes possible. Such agreement occurs when proidentity academics argue openly that biological race is a physical reality, although this admission is generally rare. It occurs much more frequently when proidentity academics deploy one of the evasive rationalizations for biological race, such as social race, race as a social reality, or race as a social construction, in support of arguing for multiracial identity. When they do this, not only do they engage in intellectual deception, but by their endorsement of long-ago-debunked biological racial categories they reify the myth of biological race in a way that keeps it alive among the general citizenry. Every instance of a scholar invoking race as a social reality—as opposed to *belief in race* as a social reality—is a step backward toward biological race rather than a step forward into enlightenment. Scholars who invoke race as a social reality do not teach the public; instead they mislead people with a bogus stamp of scholarly endorsement.

The other path—the metatheoretical approach—represents the road forward, the path upward. To take the metatheoretical path is to understand and be interested in the fact that people (including many academics) believe in the false consciousnesses of race and multirace, but to not fall prey to belief in those false consciousnesses oneself. One can then, with the requisite scholarly objectivity, study various aspects of the phenomenon from a perspective of objective intellectual clarity rather than one of biased cheerleading. We can study why people think they are multiracial without accepting that they actually are multiracial. We can study why some parents decide to indoctrinate their children to multiracial identities (or monoracial identities, for that matter), and the means they use to do so, without accepting that those children really become multiracial (or monoracial) as a result of that indoctrination. We can study the social and political effects of the multiracial identity movement on the US racial paradigm, recognizing all the while that both the paradigm and the movement are based on a biological fallacy.

And this last point is a key one, for it is our duty as scholars to strive for truth, enlightenment, and the production of factually correct information. There is a concomitant duty as well: to refute factually incorrect information when we encounter it in our fields of study. Biological race is a false consciousness that academics should be refuting at every turn. They certainly should not be invoking it directly or reifying it evasively through the subterfuges of race as a social construction or race as a social reality. And of course, since the very concept of multiracial identity is meaningless apart from an explicit notion of the sexual reproduction of children by parents from two different biological racial groups, multiracialism is a primary reifier of biological race. There should be no controversy in pointing this out.

As it paves the road forward, the metatheoretical approach must by definition take an unaccommodating and uncompromising stance toward biological race and its various reifications. Its practitioners will persist in publishing scholarly work that problematizes biological race, while continuing to examine the many ways that people manifest their belief in biological race and in the fallacy of multiracial identity. They will persevere in their efforts to build up the field of multiracial identity studies despite the seemingly steady stream of lesser-quality academic work that characterizes the proidentity point of view. Finally, they will endure in the hope that the proidentity perspective will one day join them in a dialectical engagement worthy to be called scholarly debate.

Notes

1. *Ghostbusters,* produced and directed by Ivan Reitman (Columbia Pictures, 1984), DVD.

2. Joel Williamson, *New People: Miscegenation and Mulattoes in the United States* (New York: Free Press, 1980); John G. Mencke, *Mulattoes and Race Mixture: American Attitudes and Images, 1865–1918* (Ann Arbor: UMI Research, 1979); Edward Reuter, *The Mulatto in the United States: Including a Study of the Rôle of Mixed-Blood Races Throughout the World* (Boston: Richard G. Badger, 1918; reprint, New York: Negro Universities Press, 1969).

3. Ursula Brown, *The Interracial Experience: Growing Up Black/White Racially Mixed in the United States* (Westport: Praeger, 2001); G. Reginald Daniel, *More Than Black? Multiracial Identity and the New Racial Order* (Philadelphia: Temple University Press, 2002); Marion Kilson, *Claiming Place: Biracial Young Adults of the Post–Civil Rights Era* (Westport: Bergin and Garvey, 2001); Kathleen Korgen, *From Black to Biracial: Transforming Racial Identity Among Americans* (Westport: Praeger, 1999).

4. The reference is to Hans Christian Andersen's famous 1837 children's tale, "The Emperor's New Clothes."

5. Ruth White, speech delivered at the Multiracial Solidarity March, Washington, DC, July 20, 1996.

6. National Marrow Donor Program, *Chance of a Lifetime: Questions and Answers About Unrelated Marrow Transplants* (Minneapolis, 1996).

7. I provide a fuller explication of the fallacy surrounding the argument that a federal multiracial category is a necessity for medical reasons in Rainier Spencer, *Spurious Issues: Race and Multiracial Identity Politics in the United States* (Boulder: Westview, 1999), 153–159.

8. Korgen, *From Black to Biracial,* 105.

9. Ibid.

Bibliography

Abbott, Edwin. *Flatland: A Romance of Many Dimensions.* 2nd ed. London: Seeley, 1884. Reprint, New York: Penguin, 1998.

Bradbury, Ray. *The Martian Chronicles.* New York: Bantam, 1979.

Brown, Ursula. *The Interracial Experience: Growing Up Black/White Racially Mixed in the United States.* Westport: Praeger, 2001.

Brummett, Patricia O'Donnell, and Loretta Winters. "Gang Affiliation and Self-Esteem: The Effects of a Mixed-Heritage Identity." In *New Faces in a Changing America: Multiracial Identity in the 21st Century,* eds. Loretta Winters and Herman DeBose, 335–354. Thousand Oaks, CA: Sage, 2003.

Chestang, Leon. "The Dilemma of Biracial Adoption." *Social Work* 17, no. 3 (May 1972): 100–105.

Christian, Mark. *Multiracial Identity: An International Perspective.* New York: St. Martin's, 2000.

Dalmage, Heather M. Introduction to *The Politics of Multiracialism: Challenging Racial Thinking,* ed. Heather M. Dalmage, 1–16. Albany: State University of New York Press, 2004.

———. "Protecting Racial Comfort, Protecting White Privilege." In *The Politics of Multiracialism: Challenging Racial Thinking,* ed. Heather M. Dalmage, 203–218. Albany: State University of New York Press, 2004.

Daniel, G. Reginald. *More Than Black? Multiracial Identity and the New Racial Order.* Philadelphia: Temple University Press, 2002.

———. "Multiracial Identity in Global Perspective: The United States, Brazil, and South Africa." In *New Faces in a Changing America: Multiracial Identity in the 21st Century,* eds. Loretta Winters and Herman DeBose, 247–286. Thousand Oaks, CA: Sage, 2003.

Farley, Reynolds. "Racial Identities in 2000: The Response to the Multiple-Race Response Option." In *The New Race Question: How the Census Counts Multiracial Individuals,* eds. Joel Perlmann and Mary C. Waters, 33–61. New York: Russell Sage Foundation, 2002.

Gallagher, Charles A. "Racial Redistricting: Expanding the Boundaries of Whiteness." In *The Politics of Multiracialism: Challenging Racial*

Thinking, ed. Heather M. Dalmage, 59–76. Albany: State University of New York Press, 2004.

Gans, Herbert. "The Possibility of a New Racial Hierarchy in the Twenty-First-Century United States." In *The Cultural Territories of Race: Black and White Boundaries,* ed. Michele Lamont, 371–390. Chicago: University of Chicago Press, 1999.

Ghostbusters. Produced and directed by Ivan Reitman. Columbia Pictures, 1984. DVD.

Gordon, Lewis R. "Race, Biraciality, and Mixed Race." In *"Mixed Race" Studies: A Reader,* ed. Jayne O. Ifekwunigwe, 158–165. London: Routledge, 2004.

Hayes, Peter. "Transracial Adoption: Politics and Ideology." *Child Welfare* 72, no. 3 (May–June 1993): 301–310.

Hernández, Tanya K. "'Multiracial' Discourse: Racial Classifications in an Era of Color-Blind Jurisprudence." *Maryland Law Review* 57, no. 97 (1998): 98–172.

Hurst, Fannie. *Imitation of Life.* New York: Harper, 1933.

Ifekwunigwe, Jayne O. "Introduction: Rethinking 'Mixed Race' Studies." In *"Mixed Race" Studies: A Reader,* ed. Jayne O. Ifekwunigwe, 1–29. London: Routledge, 2004.

Jacobson, Matthew F. "History, Historicity, and the Census Count by Race." In *The New Race Question: How the Census Counts Multiracial Individuals,* eds. Joel Perlmann and Mary C. Waters, 259–262. New York: Russell Sage Foundation, 2002.

Kant, Immanuel. *Critique of Practical Reason.* Translated by Lewis W. Beck. New York: Macmillan, 1985.

Kilson, Marion. *Claiming Place: Biracial Young Adults of the Post–Civil Rights Era.* Westport: Bergin and Garvey, 2001.

King-O'Riain, Rebecca Chiyoko. "Model Majority? The Struggle for Identity Among Multiracial Japanese Americans." In *The Politics of Multiracialism: Challenging Racial Thinking,* ed. Heather M. Dalmage, 177–191. Albany: State University of New York Press, 2004.

Korgen, Kathleen. *From Black to Biracial: Transforming Racial Identity Among Americans.* Westport: Praeger, 1999.

Lazarre, Jane. *Beyond the Whiteness of Whiteness: Memoir of a White Mother of Black Sons.* Durham, NC: Duke University Press, 1996.

Mathews, Linda. "More Than Identity Rides on a New Racial Category." *New York Times,* July 6, 1996, A1, A7.

Mencke, John G. *Mulattoes and Race Mixture: American Attitudes and Images, 1865–1918.* Ann Arbor: UMI Research, 1979.

Mengel, Laurie M. "Triples—The Social Evolution of a Multiracial Panethnicity: An Asian American Perspective." In *Rethinking "Mixed Race,"* eds. David Parker and Miri Song, 99–116. London: Pluto, 2001.

Moran, Rachel. *Interracial Intimacy: The Regulation of Race & Romance.* Chicago: University of Chicago Press, 2001.

Morning, Ann. "New Faces, Old Faces: Counting the Multiracial Population Past and Present." In *New Faces in a Changing America: Multiracial Identity in the 21st Century,* eds. Loretta Winters and Herman DeBose, 41–67. Thousand Oaks, CA: Sage, 2003.

Myrdal, Gunnar. *An American Dilemma: The Negro Problem and Modern Democracy.* New York: Harper and Brothers, 1944.

National Marrow Donor Program. *Chance of a Lifetime: Questions and Answers About Unrelated Marrow Transplants.* Minneapolis, 1996.

National Research Council. Committee on National Statistics. Panel on Census Requirements in the Year 2000 and Beyond. *Modernizing the U.S. Census.* Edited by Barry Edmonston and Charles Schultze. Washington, DC: National Academy Press, 1995.

———. Committee on National Statistics. *Spotlight on Heterogeneity: The Federal Standards for Racial and Ethnic Classification, Summary of a Workshop.* Edited by Barry Edmonston, Joshua Goldstein, and Juanita T. Lott. Washington, DC: National Academy Press, 1996.

Njeri, Itabari. "The Last Plantation." In *"Mixed Race" Studies: A Reader,* ed. Jayne Ifekwunigwe, 295–302. London: Routledge, 2004.

Olumide, Jill. *Raiding the Gene Pool: The Social Construction of Mixed Race.* London: Pluto, 2002.

Pabst, Naomi. "Blackness/Mixedness: Contestations over Crossing Signs." *Cultural Critique* 54 (Spring 2003): 178–212.

Parker, David, and Miri Song. "Introduction: Rethinking 'Mixed Race.'" In *Rethinking "Mixed Race,"* eds. David Parker and Miri Song, 1–22. London: Pluto, 2001.

Perry, Twila. "Race and Child Placement: The Best Interests Test and the Cost of Discretion." In *Mixed Race America and the Law: A Reader,* ed. Kevin Johnson, 343–350. New York: New York University Press, 2003.

Ramirez, Deborah. "Multicultural Empowerment: It's Not Just Black and White Anymore." In *Mixed Race America and the Law: A Reader,* ed. Kevin Johnson, 197–199. New York: New York University Press, 2003.

Reuter, Edward. *The Mulatto in the United States: Including a Study of the Rôle of Mixed-Blood Races Throughout the World.* Boston: Richard G. Badger, 1918. Reprint, New York: Negro Universities Press, 1969.

Robinson, Reginald L. "The Shifting Race-Consciousness Matrix and the Multiracial Category Movement: A Critical Reply to Professor Hernández." *Boston College Third World Law Journal* 20, no. 2 (Spring 2000): 231–289.

Rockquemore, Kerry Ann. "Deconstructing Tiger Woods: The Promise and the Pitfalls of Multiracial Identity." In *The Politics of Multiracialism: Challenging Racial Thinking,* ed. Heather M. Dalmage, 125–141. Albany: State University of New York Press, 2004.

Rockquemore, Kerry Ann, and David Brunsma. *Beyond Black: Biracial Identity in America.* Thousand Oaks, CA: Sage, 2002.

Rockquemore, Kerry Ann, and Tracey Laszloffy. *Raising Biracial Children: From Theory to Practice.* Walnut Creek, CA: Alta Mira, 2005.

Romano, Renee C. *Race Mixing: Black-White Marriage in Postwar America.* Cambridge: Harvard University Press, 2003.

Root, Maria P. P. "Five Mixed-Race Identities: From Relic to Revolution." In *New Faces in a Changing America: Multiracial Identity in the 21st Century,* eds. Loretta Winters and Herman DeBose, 3–20. Thousand Oaks, CA: Sage, 2003.

———. *Love's Revolution: Interracial Marriage.* Philadelphia: Temple University Press, 2001.

————, ed. *The Multiracial Experience: Racial Borders as the New Frontier.* Thousand Oaks, CA: Sage, 1996.

————, ed. *Racially Mixed People in America.* Newbury Park, CA: Sage, 1992.

Ropp, Steven. "Do Multiracial Subjects Really Challenge Race? Mixed Race Asians in the United States and the Caribbean." In *"Mixed Race" Studies: A Reader,* ed. Jayne Ifekwunigwe, 263–270. London: Routledge, 2004.

Rosenblatt, Paul C., Terri A. Karis, and Richard Powell. *Multiracial Couples: Black & White Voices.* Thousand Oaks, CA: Sage, 1995.

Senna, Danzy. "The Mulatto Millennium." In *Half and Half: Writers on Growing Up Biracial and Bicultural,* ed. Claudine C. O'Hearn, 12–27. New York: Pantheon, 1998.

Simon, Rita J., and Howard Altstein. *Adoption, Race, & Identity: From Infancy to Young Adulthood.* New Brunswick, NJ: Transaction, 2002.

Small, Stephen. "Colour, Culture, and Class: Interrogating Interracial Marriage and People of Mixed Racial Descent in the USA." In *Rethinking "Mixed Race,"* eds. David Parker and Miri Song, 117–133. London: Pluto, 2001.

Smedley, Audrey. *Race in North America: Origin and Evolution of a Worldview.* 2nd ed. Boulder: Westview, 1999.

Spencer, Jon M. *The New Colored People: The Mixed-Race Movement in America.* New York: New York University Press, 1997.

Spencer, Rainier. "Assessing Multiracial Identity Theory and Politics: The Challenge of Hypodescent." *Ethnicities* 4, no. 3 (2004): 357–379.

————. "Beyond Pathology and Cheerleading: Insurgency, Dissolution, and Complicity in the Multiracial Idea." In *The Politics of Multiracialism: Challenging Racial Thinking,* ed. Heather M. Dalmage, 101–124. Albany: State University of New York Press, 2004.

————. "Census 2000: Assessments in Significance." In *New Faces in a Changing America: Multiracial Identity in the 21st Century,* eds. Loretta Winters and Herman DeBose, 99–110. Thousand Oaks, CA: Sage, 2003.

————. *Spurious Issues: Race and Multiracial Identity Politics in the United States.* Boulder: Westview, 1999.

Streeter, Caroline A. "The Hazards of Visibility: 'Biracial' Women, Media Images, and Narratives of Identity." In *New Faces in a Changing America: Multiracial Identity in the 21st Century,* eds. Loretta Winters and Herman DeBose, 301–322. Thousand Oaks, CA: Sage, 2003.

Texeira, Mary Thierry. "The New Multiracialism: An Affirmation of or an End to Race As We Know It?" In *New Faces in a Changing America: Multiracial Identity in the 21st Century,* eds. Loretta Winters and Herman DeBose, 21–37. Thousand Oaks, CA: Sage, 2003.

Tizard, Barbara, and Ann Phoenix. *Black, White, or Mixed Race? Race and Racism in the Lives of Young People of Mixed Parentage.* London: Routledge, 1993.

US House Subcommittee on Census, Statistics, and Postal Personnel. Committee on Post Office and Civil Service. *Hearings on the Review of Federal Measurements of Race and Ethnicity.* 103rd Cong., 1st sess., April 14, June 30, July 29, November 3, 1993.

US House Subcommittee on Government Management, Information, and Technology. Committee on Government Reform and Oversight. *Hearings on Federal Measures of Race and Ethnicity and the Implications for the 2000 Census.* 105th Cong., 1st sess., April 23, May 22, July 25, 1997.

Wallace, Kendra. *Relative/Outsider: The Art and Politics of Identity Among Mixed Heritage Students.* Westport: Ablex, 2001.

Walsh, Eileen T. "Ideology of the Multiracial Movement: Dismantling the Color Line and Disguising White Supremacy?" In *The Politics of Multiracialism: Challenging Racial Thinking,* ed. Heather M. Dalmage, 219–235. Albany: State University of New York Press, 2004.

Wheelwright, Philip, ed. *The Presocratics.* New York: Macmillan, 1985.

White, Ruth. Speech delivered at the Multiracial Solidarity March, Washington, DC, July 20, 1996.

Williams, Kim. "Linking the Civil Rights and Multiracial Movements." In *The Politics of Multiracialism: Challenging Racial Thinking,* ed. Heather M. Dalmage, 77–97. Albany: State University of New York Press, 2004.

Williams-León, Teresa. "Check All That Apply: Trends and Prospectives Among Asian-Descent Multiracials." In *New Faces in a Changing America: Multiracial Identity in the 21st Century,* eds. Loretta Winters and Herman DeBose, 158–175. Thousand Oaks, CA: Sage, 2003.

Williamson, Joel. *New People: Miscegenation and Mulattoes in the United States.* New York: Free Press, 1980.

Wilson, Anne. *Mixed Race Children: A Study of Identity.* Boston: Allen and Unwin, 1987.

Winters, Loretta, and Herman DeBose. "The Dilemma of Biracial People of African American Descent." In *New Faces in a Changing America: Multiracial Identity in the 21st Century,* eds. Loretta Winters and Herman DeBose, 127–157. Thousand Oaks, CA: Sage, 2003.

Zack, Naomi, ed. *American Mixed Race: The Culture of Microdiversity.* Lanham: Rowman and Littlefield, 1995.

Index

Abbott, Edwin, 11, 35
Activism: antiracist, 13; multiracial, 13; question on whose behalf undertaken, 13; of white mothers, 13, 90
Adoption, transracial, 43
Affirmative action, 58
Afro-Americans: decisions on multiracial status for, 85–110; equalization of black and white genes in, 100; erasure of pasts of, 87; genetic mix in, 4; hypodescent and, 87, 90; mixed ancestry of, 85–110; multiracial vs. not multiracial, 7
American Civil Rights Institute, 107
Antimiscegenation laws. *See Loving v. Commonwealth of Virginia*
A Place for Us Ministry for Interracial Couples, 107, 116
Asian Americans, 65

Biculturalism, 27
Bradbury, Ray, 63
Brown, James, 5, 78
Brown, Ursula, 11, 12, 16, 17, 18, 22, 24, 25, 26, 28, 38, 40, 41, 42, 43, 44, 45, 51, 52, 53, 55, 56, 63, 64, 81, 108, 114
"Browning of America," 100, 101
Brummet, Patricia, 42
Brunsma, David, 42

Carew, Rod, 116, 117
Chestang, Leon, 56
Children, black/white: actions of white mothers of, 74–82; adoption by white parents, 43; challenges of racism for, 53; choosing racial identity of, 85–110; claims of special needs of, 7, 41, 52, 53, 54; in colonial era, 71, 72; culture of victimization regarding, 52; determination that hypodescent undermines ability to form clear racial identity, 41, 42; distancing of, from stigma of blackness, 91; nonsocial determination of race of, 88; parental indoctrination in multiracial identity and, 49, 74; pseudopsychology and, 42; race defined biologically for, 15; reactions to racism, 57; sociolegal invisibility of, 41; studied by psychologists, 41; taunts and, 54
Christian, Mark, 102
Civil Rights Movement, 23
Claiming Place: Biracial Young Adults of the Post–Civil Rights Era (Kilson), 11, 25
Connerly, Ward, 107
Coping skills myth, 55, 56, 62n67
Cultural: acclimation, 27; distinctions, 28; insight, 27; intimacy, 29; styles, 27
Culture: black, 30; conflating with race,

About the Book

What is multiracialism—and what are the theoretical consequences and practical costs of asserting a multiracial identity? Arguing that the multiracial movement bolsters, rather than subverts, traditional categories of race, Rainier Spencer critically assesses current scholarship in support of multiracial identity.

Rainier Spencer is director of the Afro-American Studies Program and associate professor in the Department of Anthropology and Ethnic Studies at the University of Nevada, Las Vegas.